Tipbook
Trumpet
and Trombone
Flugelhorn and Cornet

The Complete Guide

Hugo Pinksterboer

Tipbook
Trumpet
and Trombone — Flugelhorn and Cornet

The Complete Guide

HAL•LEONARD®

The Complete Guide to Your Instrument!

788.919

First edition published in 2001 by The Tipbook Company bv,
The Netherlands

Second edition published in 2009 by
Hal Leonard Books
An Imprint of Hal Leonard Corporation
7777 West Bluemound Road
Milwaukee, WI 53213

Trade Book Division Editorial Offices
19 West 21st Street, New York, NY 10010

Printed in the United States

Book design by Gijs Bierenbroodspot

Library of Congress Cataloging-in-Publication Data

Pinksterboer, Hugo.
  Tipbook trumpet and trombone, flugelhorn and cornet : the complete guide / Hugo Pinksterboer. -- 2nd ed.
    p. cm. — (Tipbook series)
  Previous ed.: Netherlands : Tipbook, 2001.
  Includes bibliographical references and index.
  ISBN 978-1-4234-6527-0 (pbk.)
  1. Brass instruments. 2. Trumpet. 3. Trombone. 4. Cornet.
    5. Flügelhorn. I. Title.
  ML933.P56 2010
  788.9'19—dc22

                          2009044807

IV

Thanks!

For their information, their expertise, their time, and their help we'd like to thank the following musicians, teachers, technicians, and other brasswind experts:

Donald R. Harrell (Kanstul, CA), Max Gastauer (B&S, Germany), Jeff Christiana and Kelly Edwards, Brock M. Scutchfield, Dean Loy, Bernd Limberg (Gewa, Germany), Frits Damrow (Conservatory of Amsterdam), Jarmo Hoogendijk (Nueva Manteca, Conservatories of The Hague and Rotterdam), Hub van Laar (Hub van Laar Trumpets & Flugelhorns), Bart van Lier (Conservatories of Amsterdam and Rotterdam), Jörgen van Rijen, Kik Boon, Luc Decock, Gerald van Dijk, Harm van der Geest, Bart Noorman, Bert Reuyl, Henk Rensink, Henk Smit, Harry Thoren, Diana Voorhof, Hans de Winter, Jacob Bakker, Paul van Bebber (First Brass), Aad Contze (Selmer/ BIN), Pieter Bukkems and Harm Roestenberg (Holton, Martin), Guus Dohmen, Harry Thoren, Gerard ten Hoedt and Jeroen Bos, Gerard Koning (Yamaha), Dirk de Moor (Musik Meyer), Bart Noorman, Jan Otten, Henk Rensink, Tom Reitsma, Jaap Ruisch (Van der Glas), Jan Slot, Richard Steinbusch (Adams), and our Tipcode artists, Ruud van de Laar and the late Louis Schuijt.

Special thanks to Jilt Jansma (author of the trombone method *Look, Listen, and Learn*) for his help in creating the trombone slide position charts, and to Angelo Verploegen for his contributions to the trumpet fingering charts.

About the Author

Journalist and musician **Hugo Pinksterboer**, author and editor of The Tipbook Series has published hundreds of interviews, articles and instrument reviews, and DVD, CD, and book reviews for a variety of international music magazines.

About the Designer

Illustrator, designer, and musician **Gijs Bierenbroodspot** has worked as an art director for a wide variety of magazines and has developed numerous ad campaigns. While searching in vain for information about saxophone mouthpieces, he got the idea for this series of books on music and musical instruments. He is responsible for the layout and illustrations of all of the Tipbooks.

Acknowledgments

Cover photo: René Vervloet
Editors: Robert L. Doerschuk and Meg Clark
Proofreaders: Nancy Bishop and René de Graaff

Anything missing?

Any omissions? Any areas that could be improved? Please go to www.tipbook.com to contact us. Thanks!

Trademarks

Trademarks and/or usernames have been used in this book solely to identify the products or instruments discussed. Such use does not identify endorsement by or affiliation with the trademark owner(s).

Contents

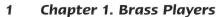

VIII

Introduction

Have you just started playing the trumpet, the trombone, the flugelhorn, or the cornet? Are you thinking about buying one of those instruments, or do you just want to learn more about the one you already have? If so, this book will tell you all you need to know. It covers buying and renting brasswind instruments, lessons and practicing, auditioning and selecting an instrument, choosing mouthpieces and mutes, as well as maintenance and tuning, the history and the family of these instruments, and much more.

Having read this Tipbook, you'll be able to get the best out of your instrument, to buy the best trumpet or trombone you can, and to easily grasp any other literature on the subject, from books and magazines to catalogs and online publications.

Basics
The first four chapters are meant for beginning players, or their parents. They explain the basics and the main characteristics of the instruments that are covered in this book, and they inform you on learning to play a brasswind instrument, practicing, and buying or renting an instrument. This information also fully prepares you to read the rest of the book.

Advanced players
Advanced players can skip ahead to Chapter 5, where you will find everything you need to know to make an informed purchase

when you're going to buy one of the instruments discussed in this book. Chapters 6 and 7 offer similar information on mouthpieces and mutes respectively. Please note that all price indications in these and other chapters are based on estimated street prices in US dollars.

Maintenance

Chapters 8 and 9 deal with maintenance, from assembly and tuning to cleaning, and related subjects. Tips on brasswind accessories are also included.

Background information

The final chapters offer basic reading material on the history of brasswind instruments, their family, the way they're made, and the main brand names that you'll come across.

Glossary and index

To make the information in this book even more accessible, there's a glossary and a complete index of terms. Two additional pages allow you to jot down all relevant data of your instruments.

Practicing, reducing stage fright, and fingerings

As an essential extra, this Tipbook provides you with special chapters on effective practicing and reducing performance anxiety. Fingering charts for trumpeters and slide position charts for trombone players are also included. Enjoy!

— **Hugo Pinksterboer**

See and Hear What You Read with Tipcodes

www.tipbook.com

In addition to the many illustrations on the following pages, Tipbooks offer you a new way to see — and even hear — what you are reading about. The Tipcodes that you will come across regularly in this book give you access to extra pictures, short videos, sound files, and other additional information at www.tipbook.com.

Here's how it works. Below the paragraph on jammed slides on page 131 is a short section marked **Tipcode TRP-019**. Type in that code on the Tipcode page at www.tipbook.com and you will see a short video that shows you how to use a cloth to remove a jammed slide. Similar videos are available on a variety of subjects; other Tipcodes will link to a sound file.

TIPCODE

Tipcode TRP-019
Here's how you can remove a jammed slide with a cloth.

XII

Repeat
If you miss something the first time, you can replay the Tipcode. And if it all happens too fast, use the pause button beneath the movie window.

Tipcode list
For your convenience, the Tipcodes presented in this book are listed on page 192.

Plug-ins
If the software you need to view the videos is not yet installed on your computer, you'll automatically be told which software you need, and where you can download it. This type of software is free. Questions? Check out 'About this site' at www.tipbook.com.

First, make your selection: Tipcode, chords and fingering charts, or the glossary.

The Tipcode window displays movies, photo series, fingering charts, chords, and explanations of the words used in this book.

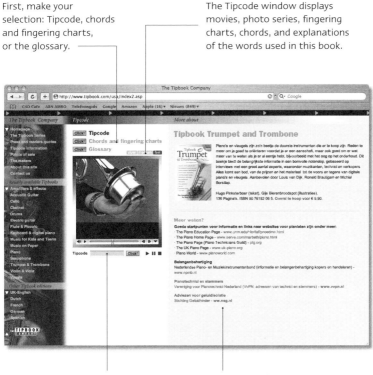

Enter a Tipcode here and click on the button. Want to see it again? Click again.

These links take you directly to other interesting sites.

XIII

Still more at www.tipbook.com

You can find even more information at www.tipbook.com.
For instance, you can look up words in the glossaries of all
the Tipbooks published to date. There are chord diagrams
for guitarists and pianists; fingering charts for saxophonists,
clarinetists, and flutists; and rudiments for drummers. Also
included are links to most of the websites mentioned in the *Want
to Know More?* section of each Tipbook.

Tipbook

Trumpet

and Trombone Flugelhorn and Cornet

The Complete Guide

1

Brass Players

Brass players play brasswind instruments, like the four types of horns discussed in this book. One of the fun things about these instruments is that you can play them in wide variety of bands and orchestras, and in many different musical styles.

If you play the guitar, you make the strings vibrate. On a drum, it's the drumheads that vibrate. And if you play a brasswind instrument, you make your lips vibrate.

Different sounds
Try closing your lips, and then blow air through them. You don't need any practice to make this sound like air escaping from a balloon, or an old motorbike, or a whole lot of other things. Likewise, you can make a brasswind instrument sound many different ways. From high to low, and from crisp, bright, and edgy to warm, soft, or full.

Trumpeters and trombonists
This is one of the things that makes brasswinds such versatile instruments. As a trumpeter or a trombonist you can play in a jazz band, a symphony orchestra, or a brass band; you can join a salsa group or a chamber orchestra, play with a mariachi band or a concert band, or in many other groups and ensembles.

Flugelhorns
The flugelhorn, which sounds fuller, warmer, and mellower than a trumpet, is mainly used in jazz and classical music. Some players specialize on the flugelhorn, but there are many trumpeters who play it as their second instrument.

TIPCODE

Tipcode TRP-002
The trumpet and the flugelhorn can be used in a wide variety of styles. Many players play both instruments. Others specialize in either one of the two.

Cornets
The sound of a cornet is somewhere between that of a flugelhorn and a trumpet. It's brighter than the first, but not as bright as the

2

latter — and it's mellower than the latter, but not as mellow as the first. Cornets are typically played in brass bands, where they're one of the main voices, and they're used in Dixieland bands and symphony orchestras, for example.

A trumpet, a British style cornet, and a flugelhorn

Orchestras and bands

There's more about the various orchestras and bands you can join as a brass player in Chapter 14 of this book.

Horn

Brasswind players have at least one thing in common: Whether they play a low-budget student instrument or a hand-crafted gem, they'll often call it their horn. Incidentally, the same word is used by saxophonists too, even though the saxophone is a woodwind instrument (see page 000).

3

Three buttons or a slide

Brass instruments look deceivingly simple, with no more than three buttons (the valves) or a slide, but that doesn't make them the easiest musical instruments to play. Still, learning a few basic songs on a trumpet or a trombone is a matter of weeks or months.

Trombone

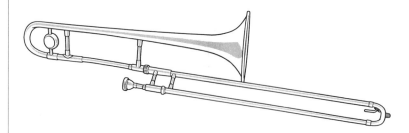

Just your instrument

On top of that, brasswind instruments are very affordable, and it won't cost you a fortune to buy a decent instrument that you can enjoy for many years. Also, brass players don't need to buy strings, reeds, batteries, heads, sticks, or any other expensive replacement parts. All you need is your instrument, a mouthpiece, a case, and the odd drop of oil. That's it!

4

2

A Quick Tour

The four instruments in this book have many things in common. That goes especially for the trumpet, the cornet, and the flugelhorn, of course. Still, a trombone looks more different from these instruments than it really is. This chapter explains the basics of these brasswinds, their key differences and similarities, and what their main parts are and what they do.

Trumpets and trombones are more alike than you might think. A trumpet is a long tube with three valves; a trombone is a long tube with an extendable slide. You need those valves or the slide to be able to play all the different notes.

A few notes

On a brass instrument without valves or a slide you can only play a limited number of different notes. You play these notes mainly by varying your lip tension. A higher tension makes your lips vibrate faster, producing a higher pitch.

TIPCODE

Tipcode TRP-003
This Tipcodes demonstrates the first five notes that you can play without using the valves.

Harmonics

The different notes that you can play this way are known as *harmonics* or *naturals*. Beginning trumpeters or trombonists can only play six or seven harmonics. That choice of notes really limits the number of songs you can play.

The first nine notes you can play on a valveless trumpet.

C4   G4   C5   E5   G5   B♭5   C6   D6   E6
(Middle C)

A little longer, a little lower

The slide of a trombone and the valves of a trumpet allow you to make the instrument a little longer, step by step. Making the

6

instrument longer makes it sound lower, a half step or half tone at a time. Each time you do so, you get access to a new series of six, seven or more notes.

Gradually longer in seven steps.

Seven steps, seven series

You can easily see that a trombone gets longer as you extend the slide. The slide has seven positions, from fully in to fully out. That means you can play seven 'series' of seven, eight or more notes. Together, those notes allow you to play anything you want.

Valves

A trumpet basically works the same way. Its three valves allow you to make the tube a little longer each time, in seven steps. Here's how.

Without valves

If you don't use the valves, the air vibrates in the main tube of the instrument only — from the mouthpiece to the valves, and from the valves directly to the bell. Without using the valves, you can play one series of harmonics or notes only.

Second valve: a half step lower

If you press the second valve, the small U-shaped tube attached to this valve is added to the instrument. This makes the tube of the trumpet slightly longer, enabling you to

No valves: air vibrating in the main tube only.

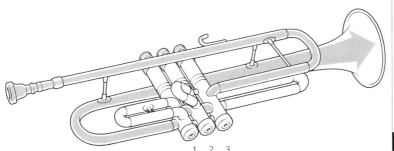

1 2 3

play a new series of notes. These notes sound *a half step lower* than the notes that you can play without using the valves.

The air in the first valve slide vibrates as well, making the instrument sound a whole step lower.

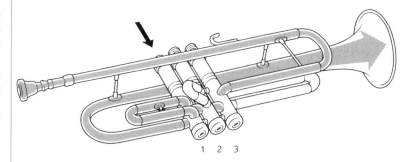

1 2 3

Tipcode TRP-004
Pressing the second valve allows you to play a series of notes that sound a half step lower, as you can see and hear in this Tipcode.

First valve: two half steps lower

The U-shaped tube of the first valve, closest to the mouthpiece, is about twice as long as the tube of the second valve. If you depress the first valve, you can play a series of notes that sound *two half steps lower* than the ones without valves.

Third valve: three half steps lower

The tube attached to the third valve is about as long as the combined tubes of the first and second valves. Using this valve allows you to play a series of notes that sound *three half steps lower* than the ones without valves.

Seven positions

Back to the trombone: A trombone slide that is fully retracted is in the *first position*. The *seventh position* means it's fully open.

Similarly, the three valves of a trumpet allow for seven 'positions'. This is shown in the table below.

trumpet valves	trombone slide position
0	first
2	second
1	third
1+2 (=3)	fourth
2+3	fifth
1+3	sixth
1+2+3	seventh

TRUMPET

So a trumpet is really a very basic instrument: a long tube with two bends, and three valves that allow you to vary its length in seven steps. If you take a closer look, there is much more to see.

Mouthpiece
Brasswinds are *lip-vibrated instruments*: You play them by vibrating your lips in the cup of the *mouthpiece*.

Leadpipe
The mouthpiece sticks into the *mouthpiece receiver*. The next piece of tubing, up till the first bend, is known as the *leadpipe* or *mouthpipe*.

Tuning slide
You tune a trumpet by pulling out the first bend of the instrument, at the end of the leadpipe. If you extend this *main tuning slide* or *tuning crook*, you make the instrument a little longer. As a result the pitch will become a little lower.

The third valve slide
If you go past the tuning slide, you get to the third valve. The piece of tubing attached to it is the *third valve slide* or *third slide*.

9

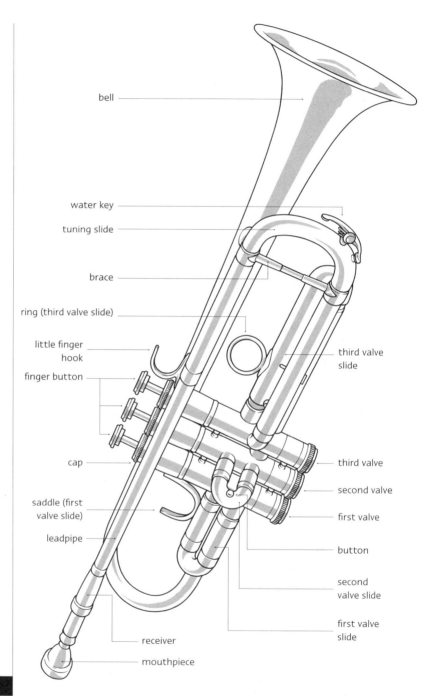

bell

water key

tuning slide

brace

ring (third valve slide)

little finger hook

finger button

cap

saddle (first valve slide)

leadpipe

third valve slide

third valve

second valve

first valve

button

second valve slide

first valve slide

receiver

mouthpiece

Fine-tuning

You can extend the third valve slide by using the attached *slide throw ring*. This allows you to fine-tune certain notes while playing.

The first valve slide

Many instruments allow for adjusting notes with the first valve slide too.

Ring or saddle

If the first valve has a valve slide or *kick slide*, you can move it with either a ring or a U-shaped *thumb hook* or *saddle*, also known as *U-pull*.

Buttons and caps

You operate the valves with your finger tips on their *finger buttons*. These are often inlaid with real or imitation mother-of-pearl.

Pistons and valve casings

The trumpet's valves are officially known as *piston valves*: In each *valve casing*, there's a *piston*, a small cylinder with holes. If the piston is up, the air passes straight through the valve, so to speak, taking the 'short route.'

Piston down

If you move the piston down, you force the air to 'make a detour' through the valve slide. This makes the tube longer, allowing for a new series of notes. The difference between the short route and the detour is clearly shown in the illustrations on page 8.

> ### Valve caps
>
> To allow the valves to move smoothly, they need to be lubricated. To do so, you can take out the pistons by unscrewing the valve caps.

The bell

The *bell* is the wide flaring part at the end of the horn. Technically, the bell also includes the last bend of the instrument: The *bell section* actually starts at the *bell tail*, just after the valve section.

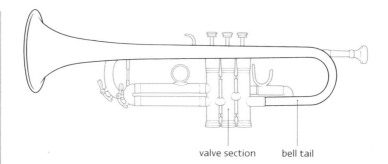

The bell starts right at the end of the valve section.

valve section   bell tail

Braces

Braces between the bell and the leadpipe make the trumpet a little sturdier. Usually there's another brace just before the tuning slide, and there may be one in the tuning slide as well.

Little finger hook

The index, middle, and ring fingers of your right hand are on the finger buttons. Your right hand little finger is in the hook on top of the leadpipe.

Water keys

As you play, the moisture from your breath will condense inside the instrument. To get rid of it, just press the *water key* and blow air through the your horn. Water keys are also known as *spit valves.*

Water keys on a trumpet (left) and a trombone (right)

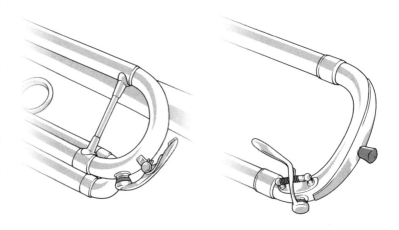

FLUGELHORN

On a flugelhorn, the bends in the tube are noticeably rounder than on a trumpet. This makes the horn look 'rounder,' and it also tends to sound 'rounder' than a trumpet.

Narrow to wide

However, the round, mellow, or velvet sound of a flugelhorn is mainly due to the fact that a flugelhorn flares out much more than a trumpet: The instruments have about the same bore size at the leadpipe, but the flugelhorn gets much wider.

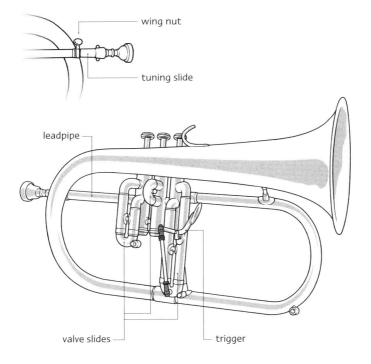

Tuning

You tune a flugelhorn by sliding its short, straight tuning slide (the receiver) in and out of the instrument. Once the instrument is in tune, you secure the tuning slide with a wing nut.

13

Vertical valve slides and triggers

Unlike trumpets, most flugelhorns have vertical first and third valve slides. You can't operate a vertical valve slide with a ring or a hook. That's why most flugelhorns have one or two *triggers* instead. If you pull the trigger's lever toward you, the slide will extend. Let the trigger go, and the slide automatically returns to its original position.

TIPCODE

Tipcode TRP-005
Here you can see and hear how the third valve slide trigger can be used to adjust the pitch of sharp notes.

Cylindrical?

Flugelhorns are clearly conical instruments. Trumpets are often referred to as cylindrical instruments, but many sections of the tubing are in fact conical. For example, many trumpets have conical leadpipes, as you can clearly see if you take a closer look. The difference in sound between flugelhorns and trumpets is mainly due to the fact that trumpets flare less than flugelhorns do: Trumpets are 'less conical.'

TIP

Lingo

Here's some flugelhorn lingo. Vertical slides are also known as French style slides. A '3rd trigger' doesn't mean there are three triggers: It's short for third valve slide trigger. The flugelhorn is also referred to as fluegel or valve bugle, *and* the word is also spelled fluegelhorn or flügelhorn.

CORNET

There are two basic types of cornet: the *American cornet*, and the *British* or *European* model. The most obvious difference is that the American cornet looks much longer. If you were to roll them both out, however, you'd see that their lengths are identical.

Same length, same key

Trumpets and flugelhorns have that same length as well, which explains why they're all B♭ instruments (see page 20–22). If an instrument would be longer, it would be in a lower key, and vice versa.

In between

The American cornet is a little closer to the trumpet, whereas the British or *short cornet* is a little closer to the flugelhorn. You can really hear that difference. The trumpet has the most cutting, bright sound, followed by the American cornet. The British cornet

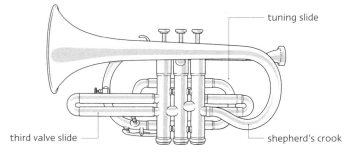

tuning slide

third valve slide

shepherd's crook

British and American-style cornets. On both models, the third valve slide sticks out some way beyond the first bend.

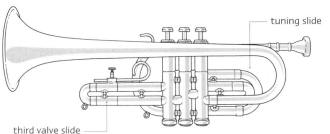

tuning slide

third valve slide

15

is a little mellower, and the flugelhorn has the smoothest tone. That said, there are trumpeters who can make their instrument sound as mellow or velvety as a flugelhorn.

Shepherd's crook
The short cornet has a small extra bend, just before the bow of the bell section. This piece of tubing looks a little like the curl of a *shepherd's crook*, and that's exactly what it's named after.

The tuning slide
On most cornets, the tube has three bends between the mouthpiece and the third valve. The tuning slide is in the second bend.

Rings and hooks
Just like trumpets, many cornets have a ring on the third valve slide and a hook on the first.

TROMBONE

When people talk about trombones they usually refer to the *tenor trombone*. This instrument is roughly twice as long as a trumpet. As a result, it also sounds quite a bit lower: one octave, to be precise (eight white keys on a piano).

Eleven feet
If you were to roll out a trombone, you'd find that it is around eight feet long. With the slide fully extended, you add nearly three feet to the instrument.

Large mouthpiece
It takes a pretty large mouthpiece to make the air vibrate throughout that whole length. The difference between a trumpet mouthpiece and a trombone mouthpiece is shown on page 80.

Two parts
The trombone consists of two main parts: the *bell section* and

the *hand slide*. The two are fixed together with a *bell lock nut*. Trombonists often use the word 'bell' to refer to the entire bell section. The large bow at the back end is the tuning slide.

Inner slide

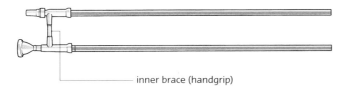

inner brace (handgrip)

The outer slide slides over the inner slide...

Outer slide

outer brace

Inner and outer slides
You operate the trombone's slide by moving the *outer slide* over the *inner slide*.

Handgrip
Your left hand holds the instrument by the *inner brace* or *handgrip*, which is attached to the inner slide. Your right hand grips the *outer brace* or *slide stay*.

Lock, knob, and water key
When you're not playing, the *slide lock* keeps the slide in place. Another security feature is the small rubber *bumper knob* on the bend of the slide, next to the water key.

Balance weight
The *bell stay* or *body brace* strengthens the bow of the bell. Many instruments have a *balance weight* or *balancer* in the bell stay. The extra weight makes it a little easier to hold the instrument without it tipping forwards.

17

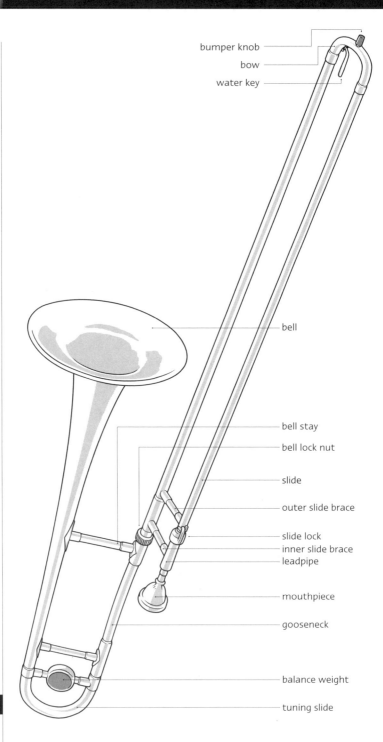

bumper knob
bow
water key

bell

bell stay

bell lock nut

slide

outer slide brace

slide lock
inner slide brace
leadpipe

mouthpiece

gooseneck

balance weight

tuning slide

Trombones with valves

There are also trombones that have either one or two valves (see pages 62–65). A trombone with two valves is a *bass trombone* (see page 54).

HOW HIGH AND HOW LOW

Most trumpeters and trombonist have a range — the distance between your lowest and your highest note — of around two and a half octaves or more. Some players can take their instruments even higher. When you are starting out, your range will be a good deal smaller.

The same

Cornets and flugelhorns have basically the same range as a trumpet, but most players can go just a little higher on a trumpet. This is mainly due to its less conical shape.

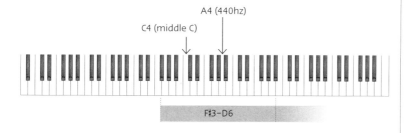

The sounding range of a trumpet, a flugelhorn, and a cornet.

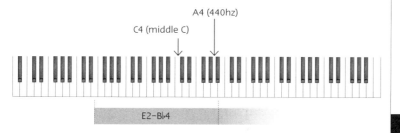

The sounding range of a trombone.

19

Different Cs

On a trumpet, you can play Middle C, a C one octave higher and a C two octaves higher. Likewise, you can play various Ds, Es, etc.

Numbers

To identify those different notes, the octaves and their notes have been numbered. Middle C is C4; the C one octave up is C5, and so on. For your reference: the lowest C on a piano is C1.

TRANSPOSING INSTRUMENTS

The most commonly used trumpet is the B♭ trumpet. Likewise, most people play B♭ cornets and flugelhorns. If you play the written note C on these instruments, the pitch you will hear is a B♭, one step below C.

When you play a B♭ trumpet, a C on paper sounds the same as a B♭ on the piano.

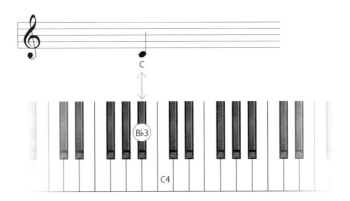

Fingerings

What this basically means, is that if a composer wants to hear a *concert pitch* B♭, he has to put a C in your chart. And if he wants to hear a D, he'll ask you to play an E.

Transposing instruments

In other words, the composer *transposes* your chart to match

20

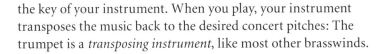
the key of your instrument. When you play, your instrument transposes the music back to the desired concert pitches: The trumpet is a *transposing instrument*, like most other brasswinds.

In G

There are also horns in other keys, and they work just the same, basically. If you have a horn in G, and the composer wants to hear a G from you, he'll write down a C. You play a C, and a concert pitch G will sound.

Advantage

One major advantage of this system? No matter the key your instrument is in, each note has its own valve combination. For example, Middle C is always played without valves, regardless of the key of the instrument.

In C

Classical musicians often play the non-transposing C trumpet. It's tubing is just a little shorter than that of a B♭ instrument, which makes it sound a whole step or whole tone higher. Because it is shorter, a C trumpet sounds not only higher, but a little brighter as well. Conversely, a B♭ trumpet sounds a little darker.

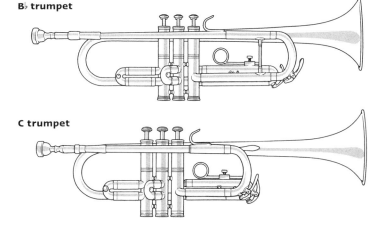

B♭ trumpet

C trumpet

The shorter C trumpet sounds brighter than the B♭ trumpet.

The trombone

Tenor trombones are B♭ instruments, just like trumpets: The

21

fundamental note of the instrument is a B♭. They're usually not considered transposing instruments, however. The concert B♭ you play with the slide completely in (first position) is usually put on paper as a B♭. There are exceptions to this rule: In brass bands, trombones are sometimes treated as a transposing instrument in B♭.

Another clef

Note that trombone parts are typically written in the F clef or bass, as opposed to the G clef or treble clef that is used for the trumpet and many other instruments.

TIP

Other pitches

There's more on brasswinds in other keys in Chapter 11, The Family.

Music on paper

Want to know more on transposing instruments or learn how easy it is to transpose parts? Then read *Tipbook Music on Paper – Basic Theory* (see page 226).

3

Learning to Play

The trumpet and the trombone aren't the very easiest instruments to start on, but you can play your first performances well within a year. The same is true for the other instruments discussed in this book.

Anybody can play any note on a piano, from high to low, without knowing how to play the instrument at all. Just hit the right key. But on a brass instrument?

Make your own notes

Brass instruments don't have a key for each note. You have to generate each pitch yourself by using three valves or a slide, the tension of your lips, and your air stream — and it does take a while to learn how to do this, and make each note sound right.

First hear it

For one thing, you need to learn to 'hear' the note you want to play in your head, before you actually play it. If not, you'll probably play a very different note.

Which one?

You also have to learn to hear which note you're actually playing, because you can't tell by looking at the instrument. (Pianists, guitarists, saxophonists, and many other instrumentalists can!) That makes playing brasswind instruments a bit like singing: You can't see which note you are singing either.

Breath control

Your lips and air stream are just as important for how you sound, and whether you're playing perfectly in tune. To be able to play long phrases, and to play in tune and with a good tone, you need to develop a proper breathing technique and air stream control. After all, playing a brass instrument involves a lot more than simply blowing air into the horn. The first long, sustained note you play on a brass instrument will probably make you feel dizzy and light-headed. Learning how to control your breath will solve this problem.

Embouchure

You also need to develop a good *embouchure*. This French term includes just about everything you do with your lips, your tongue, and all the muscles around them ('bouche' is French for mouth.) Developing proper embouchure takes time, and it takes time to keep it up too. As a brass wind player, the ability to control your lips is essential.

24

> ### Breath builders
> Musicians and manufacturers have come up with various products to help you improve your air stream and your embouchure, ranging from Brass Short Cuts (a small tube with a bell, to extend your mouthpiece) to various sorts of breath builders and air extenders.

TIP

LESSONS

If you take lessons, you'll learn about everything connected with playing the instrument, from breathing and embouchure to playing in tune, and from reading music to good posture.

Finding a teacher
Looking for a private teacher? Larger music stores may have teachers on staff, or they can refer you to one, and some players have found great teachers in musicians they have seen in performance. You can also find teachers online (see page 202). Alternatively, you may consult your local Musicians' Union, ask the band director at a high school in your vicinity, or check the classified ads in newspapers or music magazines. Professional private teachers will usually charge between thirty-five and seventy-five dollars per hour. Some make house calls, for which you'll pay extra.

Group or private lessons
Instead of taking private lessons, you can also go for group lessons, if that's an option in your vicinity. Private lessons are more expensive, but can be tailored exactly to your needs.

Collectives
You also may want to check whether there are any teachers' collectives or music schools in your vicinity. These collectives may offer extras such as ensemble playing, master classes, and clinics, in a wide variety of styles and at various levels.

25

Questions, questions

On your first visit to a teacher, don't simply ask how much it costs. Here are some other questions.

- Is an **introductory lesson** included? This is a good way to find out how well you get on with the teacher, and, for that matter, with the instrument.

- Is the teacher interested in taking you on as a student if you are just doing it **for the fun of it**, or are you expected to practice at least three hours a day?

- Do you have to make a large investment in method books right away, or is **course material provided**?

- Are you allowed to fully concentrate on the **style of music** you want to play, or will you be required to learn other styles? Or will you be stimulated to do so?

- Is this teacher going to make you **practice scales** for two years, or will you be pushed onto a stage as soon as possible?

Trumpet, flugelhorn, or cornet

The trumpet, flugelhorn, and cornet are all fairly similar to play. The cornet is often regarded as the easiest instrument for beginners. It is also a bit easier to hold than the other two. The trumpet requires more pressure too, and the flugelhorn asks for quite a lot of air.

Switching

Countless trumpeters also play the cornet or flugelhorn, and it is quite easy to switch from one instrument to another. If you have started out on a trumpet, it's a smaller step to the cornet than to the flugelhorn (and the other way around).

Trombone

A trombone is a large instrument with a large mouthpiece, and you need a good deal of air to play it. A trombone can also be difficult for children because their arms are too short to fully extend the slide, and the sixth and seventh positions are hard if not impossible to reach.

26

Smaller

This is why some teachers start children off on an alto trombone, which is a size smaller. If you switch to a tenor trombone later on, it will take some time to adjust to its different slide positions, for one thing. Other children begin on a another, smaller brass instrument, such as a trumpet or a cornet, or on a baritone (see page 143).

You may start off on an alto trombone, which is considerably smaller.

Compact trombones

Yamaha offers an alternative by making a compact trombone with an *ascending valve*. This valve eliminates the need for the sixth and seventh slide positions. Pressing it makes the instrument sound a whole step higher, allowing you to play all sixth and seventh position notes in the first and second positions respectively, with the exception of the very lowest note of the instrument, low E. The thumb button and finger ring of the instrument can be adjusted

---

Baby teeth and braces

If you happen to be losing your baby teeth, there's no need to stop playing, whatever brass instrument you play. Braces may be a problem, depending on the type of braces, on the pressure you apply with the instrument, but also on your lips and the mouthpiece you use. If you do have problems, there are various commercially available lip protectors, ranging from plastic slide-on brace guards and epoxy-based solutions to lip savers that slide over your mouthpiece — and don't forget to tell your dentist you're a brass player. Tip: There are dentists who specialize in treating horn players.

27

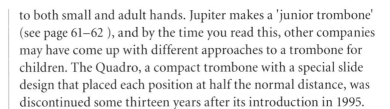

to both small and adult hands. Jupiter makes a 'junior trombone' (see page 61–62), and by the time you read this, other companies may have come up with different approaches to a trombone for children. The Quadro, a compact trombone with a special slide design that placed each position at half the normal distance, was discontinued some thirteen years after its introduction in 1995.

Other solutions
There are other solutions as well, from selecting music without sixth and seventh position notes, to special extensions that allow children to reach those positions.

PRACTICING

What goes for every instrument goes especially for wind instruments: It's better to practice half an hour every day than for four hours once a week. This is especially true for your embouchure. Professionals often notice a reduced control of the instrument when they stay away of their horn for no more than a single day.

Your ear
As a horn player, you'll also need to train your ear, because it's up to you to make sure every note you play is perfectly in tune. If you play a lot, your ear will improve pretty much by itself, as will your ability to play in tune.

Practicing tips
Chapter 15 shows you a wide variety of general tips on how to make your practice sessions both effective and entertaining. Below are some specific tips for horn players.

The neighbors
For many centuries, brasswinds have been used to wake up soldiers. Their sheer volume potential has a major drawback too, however. Here are a few tips to help you practice without bothering housemates and neighbors.

Practice mutes

A practice mute, available for some thirty to fifty
dollars, closes off the bell of your instrument.
One or more tiny holes allow very little sound to
come though, generally not disturbing anyone
outside the room you're in. On the downside,
practice mutes force you to adjust your playing:
You will need to blow harder, because of the
small holes, and the mute makes the pitch go up
slightly. Most teachers will tell you not use such
mutes routinely.

*A practice
mute.*

Peacemaker

The Peacemaker is a special practice mute with plastic tubes and
earplugs that direct the sound of the instrument to your ears,
without changing the horn's blowing characteristics.

Silent Brass

The Yamaha Silent Brass costs about six times as much, but it goes
a step further. The system consists of a plastic mute with a built-in
microphone, a small amplifier, and a pair of headphones. The amp
has an input for a CD player or another sound source, so you can
play along with prerecorded music. You can also hook up a second
Silent Brass, or a home keyboard, for instance, allowing you to

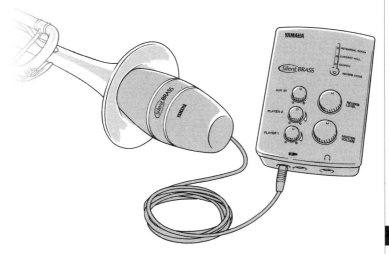

*Practice mute
with built-in
microphone
and amplifier
(Yamaha).*

29

play with a friend or your teacher. A built-in reverb adds a bit of space and life to the sound.

Fixed practice times

If you want to play without a practice mute, and neighbors or housemates are bothered by your playing, it may be enough to simply agree to fixed practice times. If you really play a lot, it may be better to insulate a room. Even a closet can be large enough. There are books available on sound insulation, you can ask around to find people who sound-proofed a room before, or you can hire a specialized contractor to do the job. Of course, it may be easier to find a practice spot outside your home.

Your own ears

If you play in a small room or with a loud band, seriously consider protecting your ears. The most basic ear plugs make it difficult to play, because they simply stop up your ears so you don't hear yourself play anymore. More expensive protectors usually don't make your instrument (or the band) sound as if it were in another room. The best and most expensive solution is too get set of custom-made ear protectors with a choice of filters, or even with adjustable filters. These filters allow you to go for maximum protection while you're still able to hear yourself play — and you should, if you want to play in tune.

Listen and play

One final tip for this chapter: Try to visit as many concerts and performances as you can. One of the best ways to learn to play is seeing other musicians at work. Living legends or local amateurs — every concert's a learning experience. And the best way to learn to play? Play a lot!

4

Buying a Brass Instrument

You can buy a decent trumpet, trombone, flugelhorn or cornet at an affordable price, but you may also spend ten thousand dollars or more. This chapter will give you an idea of what everything costs and the best places to go to buy an instrument, new or secondhand.

You can get a brand new trumpet for as little as two or three hundred dollars, and that includes a mouthpiece and a case. Prices for reliable, good-sounding intermediate instruments that you can enjoy for many years, typically start around six hundred dollars. The same goes for flugelhorns, cornets, and trombones, though the most affordable models of these instruments will usually cost a little more than a low-budget trumpet.

Pro instruments

Instruments with a 'professional' label start around fifteen hundred dollars, while most professionals actually use horns that cost between two and four thousand. The most expensive models on the market are well over ten grand, but only few companies makes instruments in this price range.

Looking and playing

Professional brasswind instruments look pretty much the same as the least expensive models. To *see* the differences you need to take a close look. To *hear* the differences you need to be a fairly experienced player. So what do you pay for when spending more money?

Better quality

Compared to student models, more time and care is devoted to professional instruments. As a result, they sound better, they're easier to play, and they last longer. More work is done by hand, from hammering the bell to hand-lapping the pistons and the slides, aiming for an airtight seal and a perfectly smooth operation.

More expensive materials

More money also buys you higher quality materials, a bell made of a special alloy, or a silver-plated or gold-plated instrument. Better materials may also allow for easier repairs.

Poor quality

The quality of budget instruments can be quite amazing, offering good sound and playability for a very reasonable price. Nevertheless, you may come across low-budget instruments you'd better not buy, because they'll never really play in tune or sound

TIP

More choices

The more you spend, the more choices you usually have, too. More expensive instruments may come with a selection of different leadpipes, tuning slides or bells, for instance, so that you can tailor the instrument to your preferences. There are companies that make a single type of trumpet in dozens of variations.

good, or because the pistons don't move as easily as they should or don't provide an airtight seal for an extended period of time.

Another player

To hear how good an instrument is, you need to be able to play quite well. That's unlikely to be the case if you're buying your first one. So take someone with you who can play, or go to a shop that has versatile and enthusiastic brass players on staff, and invite them to play various instruments for you, and to tell you about their differences.

TIP

On approval

Some stores allow you to take an instrument on approval, so that you can assess it at your leisure, both at home and in rehearsals or performances. This is more common with pro-level instruments than with student models, and you are more likely to be offered this opportunity if you're a good player than if you are choosing your first trumpet or trombone.

NEW AND PRE-OWNED INSTRUMENTS

You're always best off buying your instrument in a store where the salespeople really know what they're talking about. That's the best

33

way to make sure that you will end up with an instrument that matches your level of playing, your style, your personal taste, and your budget.

Fast repairs
You may also consider buying in a place that employs a brasswind technician, so your instrument doesn't have to be shipped for repairs.

Pre-owned instruments
You can find pre-owned instruments in music stores, but they're also available online, or in the classified sections in newspapers or music magazines, for example. If you buy an instrument from a private party, you may end up paying less than in a store.

In a music store
Still, buying a pre-owned instrument in a music store does have some major advantages. The instrument will probably have been checked and adjusted, it may come with a warranty, and you can go back if you have any questions. Also, you may be able to choose between a number of instruments, or compare them with various new horns. Another advantage is that a reputable store will never charge you much more than an instrument is worth. Private sellers might, either because they don't know better or because they think you don't.

TIP

A second opinion
If you go to buy a used horn, it's even more important to take along an advanced player who knows about the instrument, especially if you're going to buy privately. Otherwise you might turn down a decent horn just because it doesn't look good, or get saddled with one that looks great but isn't worth its price. Technical tips for buying pre-owned instruments begin on page 72.

Appraisal

34

If you want to be sure you're not paying too much, get the

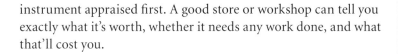
instrument appraised first. A good store or workshop can tell you exactly what it's worth, whether it needs any work done, and what that'll cost you.

Buying online

You can also buy musical instruments online or by mail-order. This makes it impossible to compare instruments. Online and mail-order companies usually do offer a return service for most or all of their products, however: If you're not happy with your purchase, you can send it back within a certain period of time. Of course the instrument should be in new condition when you return it.

RENTING

Rather than buying an instrument you can rent one. Expect to pay around some twenty to forty dollars a month. Usually, there's a minimum rental period — three months, for instance, or a school year. The rental fee is usually set as a percentage of the retail price of the instrument.

The basics

It is impossible to provide a detailed description of the infinite amount of different plans, terms, and conditions you will likely encounter when you decide to rent an instrument. But here are the basics:

- Many rental plans are actually **rent-to-own plans**: The instrument is yours once the periodic payments you've made equals the list price. Note that this list price will usually be higher than what you would have paid had you just bought the instrument outright — which explains why most of these plans are interest free.

- Most of these rent-to-own or **hire-purchase plans** also have an option to buy the instrument before you're fully paid up; if you choose to buy the instrument, your rent paid to date will usually be applied to the instrument.

35

- With a **lease plan** — also known as a straight rental plan or **rent-to-rent plan** — you simply keep paying rent until you return the instrument. Rates are usually lower on these plans than those of rent-to-own plans. With these plans, renting for a long period of time will be, of course, more expensive than buying the instrument.

Maintenance and insurance

Maintenance is usually included in the rental fee, but some plans offer it as a separate expense. The main thing is to make sure you don't have to worry about it. Insurance may be included as well. Make sure you understand what is and isn't covered under your lease or rental plan.

- Does the fee **include** instrument set-up, maintenance, and finance or bank charges?

- If **insurance** is included, does it also cover theft and loss?

- Do you get a **replacement** instrument if yours needs maintenance?

- Do you have to pay an origination fee, an application fee, or a deposit? These **fees** are usually non-refundable; they often may be applied to the rental, however.

- Always ask if you get a new or a used (rental-return) instrument.

- Is there a **reconditioning fee**, a stocking fee, or a depreciation fee when you return the instrument?

- Note that stores may ask for a **deposit** or require your credit card details.

AND FINALLY

What you consider the best horn may well be the one your favorite musician is playing. Does that mean you should buy one like it? Yes, to a point, as long as you don't expect to sound the same because of that instrument. Great musicians tend to sound like

36

themselves no matter which instrument they play, just like two musicians won't sound much the same when playing the same horn. In other words, it is you that makes the sound, and finding the right horn is basically a matter of searching for an instrument and a mouthpiece that will help promote the tone you're after.

Brochures and online sources

If you want to be well informed before you go out to buy or rent an instrument, there's a lot of reading material to digest. Check out the websites of the companies listed in Chapter 13, and other online sources, as well as brasswind catalogs and brochures, including the price lists that come with them.

Books and magazines

Additionally, there are several other books on the subject, as well as various magazines that offer reviews and other articles on the instrument, as well as on mouthpieces, mutes, and other related products. Information on these additional resources can be found on pages 199–202.

Fairs

One last tip: If a music trade fair or brasswind convention is being held anywhere near you, go and check it out. Besides being able to try and compare a considerable number of instruments, you will also have the chance to meet plenty of product specialists, as well as numerous fellow horn players who can provide information and inspiration.

5

A Good Instrument

You can get lacquered, silver-plated, and even gold-plated horns. Instruments with different bell sizes and bores, with rings or triggers, or with special tuning slides, and so on. This chapter tells you all about those differences and how they do or don't influence the sound of the instrument, or its playability.

Tips on auditioning horns, comparing them by ear, are covered in this chapter too, as well as technical tips for buying pre-owned instruments.

The first main section of this chapter focuses on the different parts of the instruments and how they affect their sound and playability. If you prefer to choose a horn using your ears only, then go straight to the tips on page 53 and onwards.

Lacquer

Bare, untreated brass makes your hands smell, and it tarnishes very easily. That's why brass instruments are usually finished with a high-gloss (epoxy) lacquer. Most manufacturers use either clear or gold lacquer, the latter with a very slight golden hue. Matte-finished horns are also available.

TIP

> ### Raw brass
> *Contrary to what you might think, unfinished instruments that show raw, unpolished brass, are usually hand-made and very expensive.*

Silver-plated

Silver-plated instruments are typically a bit more expensive, and you have to polish them more often. On the other hand, a silver plating outlasts a lacquer finish. A silver-plated trumpet will soon cost seventy-five to a hundred dollars more than an identical lacquered instrument. Of course, not all instruments are available in both finishes.

Sound

A lacquer finish is much thicker than a silver plating, which explains why lacquered instruments are usually said to sound a little warmer, smoother, mellower, or less bright: The lacquer finish reportedly mutes the sound ever so slightly. Most musicians can't tell the difference in blindfold tests, though. In fact, the difference between two 'identical' trumpets with the same finish may easily be bigger.

Gold-plated

There are several gold-plated instruments around too. The extra money buys you a sound that can be described, again, as a little

40

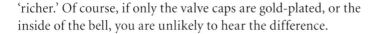

'richer.' Of course, if only the valve caps are gold-plated, or the inside of the bell, you are unlikely to hear the difference.

Nickel-plated

Nickel-plated trumpets, which are said to sound a little shallower and less expressive, are rare nowadays. Some parts may still be nickel-plated, though. Nickel looks different than silver: It has a slightly 'harder' shine. It also costs less, it is easier to maintain, and it has roughly the same life expectancy. Its main drawback is that many people are allergic to it.

Different looks

Some horns feature no less than three types of metal, and you may be looking at a yellow brass instrument with a gold brass bell and nickel-plated slides, for instance. Other companies make horns with a matte, brushed silver plating, a brushed brass finish, a black nickel-plating, or other finishes. Brightly colored instruments, available in black, red, blue, and other shades, are popular mainly in the US.

Trim

The instrument's *trim* includes the bottom and top valve caps, valve stems, water keys, finger buttons, and other replaceable parts. Some brands offer trim kits, which allow you to enhance the looks of your horn with gold-plated parts, for example.

BELL MATERIAL

Quite often, the bell material will look slightly different from the rest of the instrument, indicating that a different type of brass has been used; brass containing more copper, for instance. This does more than enhancing the looks of the instrument; it influences the sound as well. On more expensive instruments you can often choose from a variety of bell materials.

Darker, warmer, and redder

Red brass bells, with a relatively high copper content, tend to make

41

TIP

> ## Brass: yellow, rose, gold, and red
>
> *Most brass instruments are made of an alloy called* yellow
> brass, *which mainly contains zinc and (around seventy
> percent) copper. There are several names for brass with a
> higher copper content. Some companies call it* gold brass,
> *while others use the name* rose brass. *If the copper content is
> even higher, it's typically called* red brass. *Not all companies
> charge higher prices for the additional copper.*

or a warm, rich sound and to allow for a wide variety of tone
colors. Some musicians also find that the extra copper makes
the instrument respond a little faster. The same can be heard on
beryllium copper bells, for example. This lighter weight material is
also claimed to increase projection and brilliance.

Silver, bronze, or glass
Bells come in other materials too. A solid silver bell supposedly
generates a much brighter sound, for example, and there are even
trumpets with glass bells — but they're very rare.

Engraved
The brand name is almost always engraved or pressed into the bell.
You may find ornamental engravings there too, which may raise
the price of the horn some fifty to five hundred dollars or more,
depending on the price range of the instrument. Some companies
offer a choice of patterns.

THE BORE

If you pinch the end of a garden hose, you get a powerful, fierce
jet of water. Wind instruments work in much the same way. The
narrower a tube is, the 'fiercer' or edgier the sound becomes. The
inside diameter of the tube is known as the *bore*.

42

Diameter

Instrument makers often state the size of an instrument's bore. On trumpets, this bore size is usually measured at the second valve slide. Trumpet bores typically range from around 0.455" (11.56 mm) to about 0.468" (11.9 mm). When you play instruments with decidedly different bore sizes, you can soon tell that these differences are much bigger than they may appear on paper.

Medium-large

In order to play a trumpet with a large bore, you need a good embouchure and good breath control. A very small bore requires an experienced player too. Most trumpets have a bore size of about 0.460" (11.68 mm). Such a 'medium-large' bore is a good choice for beginners as well.

Larger bore

What is the effect of a larger bore?

- A larger bore helps you to create a **larger sound**: bigger, more open, and a little mellower, warmer, or darker.

- It also makes for a free-blowing horn with **plenty of volume**, though it's trickier to play very softly.

- A larger bore makes it slightly easier to **influence the tone** or **timbre** of the instrument, as well as its pitch. Note that this can make it harder to play the instrument in tune!

- Large-bore horns tend to **blend very well** with other instruments. Combined with the above, this explains why large-bore instruments are often used in symphony orchestras.

Smaller bore

A smaller bore has the opposite effect.

- Basically, a smaller bore gives a lighter, edgier, or **brighter sound**.

- You can do less to influence the tone — it's **harder to color the sound** — but it's also easier to play in tune, as pitch won't vary as much as with a larger bore.

- **Low notes** are harder to play.

43

- A smaller bore may give you **less volume**, but the sound will often project better. This explains why it doesn't blend as easily as a larger-bore instrument.

How big?

Some manufacturers indicate the bore size with figures. Others use the terms small, medium, and large, for example. Should bore sizes be given in millimeters, convert them to inches by dividing them by 25.4 (e.g., 11.73mm ÷ 25.4 = 0.462").

Trombone bores

Trombonists often start on an instrument with a relatively small bore, usually 0.485" or 0.490". A large-bore instrument (0.547") requires more air support than a beginning player will be able to supply. Bass trombones are a little wider still (0.562"–0.578").

Dual-bore trombones

On trombones with a *dual bore*, the first inner tube of the slide (*upper slide tube*) is less wide than the second (*lower slide tube*). Popular combinations are 0.525"/0.547" and 0.547"/0.562".

The effect

The narrower upper tube makes the instrument play like a smaller-bore horn, while the wider lower tube gives you the bigger sound of a wider bore instrument. The increasing bore, from tube to tube, also makes the instrument a little more 'conical.' This results in a warmer, mellower sound, compared to a regular *straight bore* trombone.

TIP

Dual-bore to larger-bore

Dual-bore trombones are sometimes used as an in-between step to a larger-bore instrument.

Gooseneck

Another part where the bore may vary is the first piece of tubing of the bell section, known as the *gooseneck* (see page 61). Some companies offer goosenecks with a selection of different bore sizes.

44

TIP

> ### Dual-bore trumpets
> *There are dual-bore trumpets too. The increasing diameter of these instruments has the same effect as a conical bore, so — again — it makes for a warmer, darker sound.*

Shape

Two instruments that have the same bore size may nonetheless sound and play very differently. Why? For one thing, the bore size only indicates the diameter of the tube at a certain point. The sound of the instrument, however, is influenced by the bore of the entire instrument, i.e., the way the tubing tapers from the start of the mouthpiece receiver to the bell's rim. The different types of tapers or flarings aren't always easy to see, but you can easily hear them, and you can feel them too, when you play.

Less conical

An example would be that American-made flugelhorns often sound a little brighter than European models, because the American models are less conical: They often start a little wider, and they're less wide at the bell.

THE BELL

Both the bell size and the flare of the bell have an influence on the sound, as well as on how freely the horn blows.

How big

The bell of a trumpet or cornet is usually no bigger than 5" (12.7 cm) in diameter, while most flugelhorn bells are between 6" and 6.75". Tenor trombone bells may range from 7" to 9", and many bass trombones come with a 10" bell. To preserve the round shape and protect the edge of the bell, most bells have a *wire reinforced rim*.

Taper

Some bells flare only toward the very end of the instrument (slow

45

taper). On other models the flare begins sooner. The latter shape is known as a gradual taper or, contradictory as it may sound, a fast taper. The more gradual the taper, the more the bell will behave like a large one, making for a warmer and darker tone, a bigger sound, and easier low notes. A less gradual taper will make for a more controllable, brighter-sounding instrument, just like a smaller bell, or an instrument with a smaller bore.

The outer line shows a slow taper; the inner line is a fast taper.

Six bells
In their professional series, some brands offer six or more different bell shapes, each with a different taper, for the same trumpet.

One-piece bells
More expensive instruments often have a one-piece bell, made of a single sheet of brass (see Chapter 12). A two-piece bell is less expensive to make, but a one-piece bell is said to make for a brighter-sounding, more responsive instrument and increased projection. One-piece bells are also referred to as *solid* or *seamless bells*. Bells with a soldered bell bead tend to produce a more focused sound with a lot of core (fundamental).

Tunable bells
Some expensive trumpets can be tuned with the bell. These *tuning bells* or *tunable bells* can be extended at the bell tail, at about an inch after the exit of the first valve (see the illustration on page 12).

46

Pros and cons

Supporters of the tunable bell concept say that this feature
enhances the tone of the instrument: Getting rid of the tuning
slide (or being able to leave it all the way in) reduces the
turbulence in the instrument, so to speak. Critics, on the other
hand, claim that horns with a tunable bell don't tune properly.
To keep everybody happy there are trumpets that feature both a
tunable bell and a tuning slide.

Different bells

If you can tune the instrument with its bell, you can also replace
the bell. This allows you to use a red brass one if you need a
warmer sound, for example, or a solid silver bell for lead playing.

No fixed braces

A tunable bell doesn't allow for fixed braces between the bell
and the leadpipe. This makes the instrument slightly more
vulnerable.

TIP

Wall thickness

The thickness of the wall also plays a role in the timbre of the
instrument. Some bells have a *variable wall thickness*, meaning that
the material gets thinner towards the bell rim. This is said to con-
tribute to a fuller, richer sound. *Double buffing* makes for a slightly
thinner bell, often with a thickness between two standard gauges.

The sound of the bell

If you flick a fingernail against the bell of an instrument, you can
hear what it sounds like. Some say that this tells you a lot about
how the whole instrument sounds. Others disagree, stating that
there are awful horns with great-sounding bells, and just as many
fine instruments with bells that don't sound good at all.

Upbell

If you like the looks, you can also get yourself an instrument with
an upturned bell, known as an *upbell*, such as the instrument that
the late jazz trumpeter Dizzy Gillespie always played. Reportedly,

47

the design was created by accident when somebody fell or stepped on Gillespie's instrument, bending the bell upwards as he did. Gillespie commented that he could hear himself better with the bell at an upward angle. Some 'convertible' instruments are supplied with both a regular bell and an *upturn bell* or upbell.

THE LEADPIPE

You hear less about leadpipes than about bells, mainly because the differences in leadpipe models are smaller. So small, in fact, that you can barely see them. But they're there. That's why some instruments come with interchangeable leadpipes, featuring different tapers and materials such as red brass, nickel, or silver.

Flare
Like bells, there are leadpipes with slower or faster tapers. A more gradual taper will yield a warmer sound, and vice versa. Also, leadpipes may have larger or smaller bores, with basically the same effect as the bore size of the entire instrument. Some brands offer special *multi-tapered leadpipes* or step-bore designs, their exact effect depending on their dimensions.

TIP

> ### Three choices
> On some trumpets you can choose from two, three, or more different leadpipes. You do need to make that choice in advance, because you can't change them yourself. On trombones you usually can.

Material
The leadpipe's material is not of the greatest importance to the sound, but it does affect how long the leadpipe will last. For example, brass with a higher copper content (i.e., rose brass, red brass, or gold brass) is less susceptible to the corrosive effect of saliva. It also promotes a slightly darker and sweeter tone.

Reversed leadpipe

The smoother the path from the mouthpiece to the bell, the smoother the tone can be. That's why many instruments have a *reversed leadpipe*: The tuning slide doesn't slide into the leadpipe, but over it. As a result, the vibrating air column in the instrument is not disturbed by the small step at the beginning of the tuning slide. The same solution is referred to as a *reversed tuning slide*, which actually is a more accurate name.

Easier to play

Trumpets with reversed leadpipes are said to be easier to play, or to be easier to play in tune. Other players prefer to have that bit more blowing resistance, or they simply prefer playing a regular instrument for any other reason. Trumpets with a reversed leadpipe are available in just about all price ranges. In some series it's offered as an option.

Adjustable gap

Dutch brass wind maker Adams produces professional instruments that allow you to adjust the blowing resistance to your embouchure by altering the length of internal gap between the mouthpiece and the leadpipe. Pitch changes as a result of changing the gap can simply be compensated for with the tuning slide.

TUNING SLIDE

Tuning slides come in two basic models. One is a little rounder; the other a little more angular. Some expensive trumpets come with one of each.

Single-radius, dual-radius

The round model is called a *single-radius tuning slide*, while the model with the angular crook is usually referred to as a *dual-radius* or *square-bend tuning slide*, among other names.

The difference

Most players consider the single-radius, rounded model easier

49

to play, boasting a more unrestricted, open feel. They also say it sounds 'rounder', just as it looks rounder. With the angular or square design, the instrument supposedly responds a little better, and high notes are easier to hit. Of course, not everyone agrees — if only because not everyone tries the same slides on the same trumpets. Also, a dual-radius model may work great on one trumpet, while another horn may sound better of be easier to play using a single-radius slide.

A dual-radius (left) and a single-radius tuning slide.

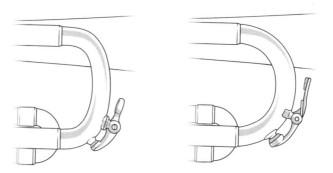

Ovate tuning slides
Ovate tuning slides are asymmetrical, with two different curves, like the egg shape they're named after ('ovum' is Latin for egg). This design is said to create a more open feel and improve intonation (see page 68), while it is also claimed to reduce piston pop, among other things. If you want to be sure about the effect that the shape of a tuning slide has for you, simply try different types of slide on one horn! Of course, you need to be at least a decent player to be able to appreciate the differences.

Braces and sound
Some tuning slides have one or even two reinforcing braces. The added weight also contributes to the sound (see page 53).

Trombones
The bend at the end of a trombone slide can also be angular or rounded. The shape does have less effect on the sound than that of the tuning slide of the instrument (see above).

50

WATER KEYS

Most water keys are very basic, reliable 'see-saw' keys with a spring and a small cork, but there are some small variations. For example, the cork can be replaced by a rubber insert shaped to fill the hole of the water key. Again, this helps reduce the turbulence in the instrument.

Amado

Other manufacturers prefer to use the Amado water key. It's less prone to leakage, as it has no cork, and its looks are quite modest, compared to a traditional water key. Amado water keys are also said to reduce the instrument's playing resistance.

 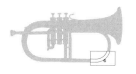

An Amado water key.

First-valve water key only

Some instruments have a first-valve water key only. On low-budget instruments, this is just to save money. When an expensive instrument has no third valve water key, this is often marketed as a way to improve the sound and intonation of the horn. Either way, such an instrument requires you to remove the third slide (or a separate crook on that slide) to get rid of the moisture.

HEAVY OR LIGHT

Not all trumpets weigh the same, and there are lighter and heavier trombones as well. Light-weight instruments tend to have a somewhat lighter and livelier sound, they are lighter to play, and they have a quicker response than heavy-weight models. This

51

typically makes them popular among jazz or Latin musicians, for example. Weight differences can be traced back mainly to the wall thickness of the tubing, but there are other ways to make an instrument heavier too.

Wall thickness

Professional instruments may be available in different wall thicknesses, e.g., 0.018" /0.45 mm or 0.020"/ 0.50 mm for trumpets.

Heavier

Heavy-weight instruments tend to have a 'heavier', thicker, richer, darker, and more focused tone than thin-wall versions. They allow you to play high notes at high volumes without the sound distorting or getting edgy or metallic. On the other hand, the heavier an instrument is, the harder work it is to play it.

The braces between leadpipe and bell may run straight or diagonal.

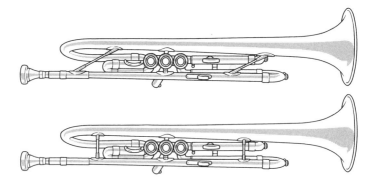

Outdoor use

Choosing heavier or lighter instruments is not about personal preference only, according to various makers. For example, thick-wall horns tend to be the preferred choice for playing outdoors, because they promote a linear projection and a one-dimensional sound. Thin-wall instruments allow players to color their tone, which is less relevant for general outdoor use. Adding weight to an instrument makes it less flexible.

Braces

Rather than using heavier tubing, extra mass can be supplied by adding parts to the instrument. Some instruments have a double leadpipe (twin tubes), or extra heavy finger hooks and rings, for instance, but adding braces or using diagonal braces (which need to be longer) helps as well.

Heavy caps

You can add weight to your instrument yourself too. One example would be to fit your instrument with extra-heavy (weighted) *bottom valve caps*, available in different sizes and weights. Some instruments com with an alternative set, so you can take your pick. Similar and alternative add-on weights are available for other horns as well. Conversely, some trombones have a removable balance weight — but this weight has more effect on the balance, as its names suggests, than on the sound of the instrument.

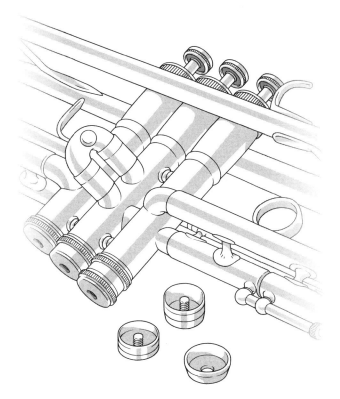

Trumpet with inter-changeable bottom caps (Conn).

53

Heavy all over

Monette, Courtois, and a few other brands make extremely heavy, expensive trumpets, that weigh nearly twice as much as standard instruments, with double-wall bells, heavy-wall tubing, and other special features.

An extra-
heavy
trumpet with
a double-wall
bell, centering
sound plates,
and other
features
(Courtois
Evolution).

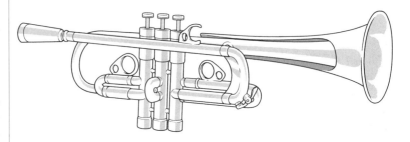

Mouthpieces

Adding mass to your mouthpiece has a similar effect, as you can read on pages 90–91.

VALVE SLIDES

Trigger on
the third
valve slide of
a flugelhorn.
Moving the
lever toward
you extends
the slide.

On most trumpets and cornets you can fine-tune certain notes with the first and third valve slides. On most flugelhorns, only the third valve slide is adjustable. If you're a trombone player, you may want to skip the following section, and move on to page 60.

Too high

Trumpets, cornets, and flugelhorns all have a few notes that normally sound a little *sharp* (too high). You can lower those notes by moving the third valve slide out a little. Why not simply make that tube a little longer? Because that would make other notes sound *flat* (too low).

Ring

An adjustable third valve slide ring can be set to accommodate shorter (children's) fingers. It's usually found on student instruments only.

54

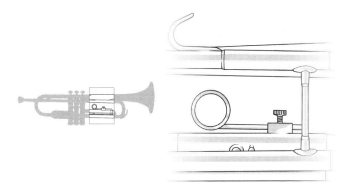

An adjustable finger ring on the third valve slide.

Security

If you move the third slide out too far, it can slip off of the instrument. A *slide stop* prevents that. Some slide stops are adjustable, so you can set the distance the slide is allowed to travel.

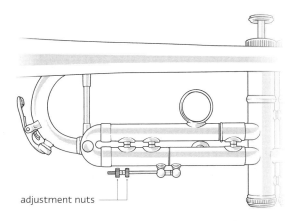

adjustment nuts

A third valve slide with an adjustable slide stop.

First valve slide

Many instruments have either a ring or a hook on the first valve slide as well, and on some instruments it's an option.

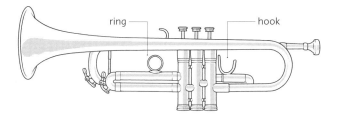

ring   hook

A ring on the third valve slide; a hook or saddle on the first.

55

Lipping up

Some players think you shouldn't use the first valve slide at all: First valve notes should be adjusted with your embouchure only ('lipping up' or 'lipping down'). Don't worry about all this if you just started playing: You usually get into fine-tuning only after a couple of years.

Second valve slide

The second slide, short as it is, isn't used for fine-tuning. It usually has a small button or *pull* that makes it easier to take it off for cleaning purposes.

Flugelhorns

Because of its conical shape, the pitch of a flugelhorn is easier to adjust with your embouchure. This is why many flugelhorns come without adjustable slides. If there's just one adjustable slide, it's the longest one, i.e., the third.

Trigger on the third valve slide of a flugelhorn. Moving the lever toward you extends the slide.

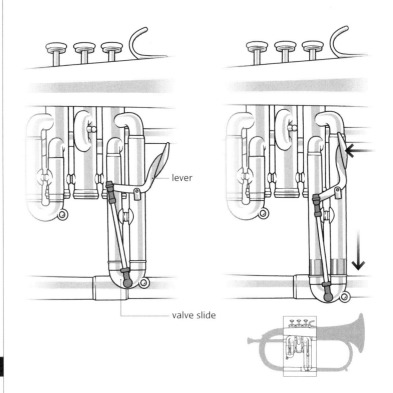

lever

valve slide

Triggers on trumpets

Some trumpeters prefer a trigger to the traditional ring or a hook; especially on the first slide, because this one is a little harder to shift with your thumb. If you can choose, getting an instrument with a trigger can easily cost an additional hundred fifty dollars. Confusing: Some call a regular valve slide a 'trigger' too, but it isn't really one.

TIP

Nickel silver and brass

To make slides slide as smoothly as they should, various combinations of alloys are used. A popular combination is nickel silver for the inside tubes, and brass for the outer tubes. Nickel silver is also used for mouthpiece receivers: The alloy helps to prevent your mouthpiece from getting stuck.

Additional slides

Some instruments come with one or more extra valve slides or tuning slides, which allows them to be used in more than one key: For example, you can turn a C trumpet into a B♭ instrument by using longer slides (see also page 138).

PISTON VALVES

Most trumpets, cornets and flugelhorns have piston valves, in which a piston moves up and down. This piston is a tube through which three tubular holes (*ports* or *portholes*) run diagonally.

Up and down

If a valve is in the 'up' position, the air will take the shortest possible path, straight through port number one. If you depress the valve, the air will be diverted through the second porthole, around the valve slide and back out through the third port. Want to see how it works? Remove the second valve slide, and take a look inside while depressing the second valve.

57

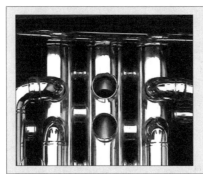

Tipcode TRP-007

Remove the second valve slide to see what happens inside when depressing the valve.

Top or bottom

In the past, piston valves were usually *bottom-sprung*: The spring that brings the valve back up was below the piston, at the bottom of the valve casing. Most modern instruments are *top-sprung*. This *top-action* design usually has enclosed springs, so they won't jump out when you remove the pistons. Today, bottom-sprung or *bottom-action* valves are found mainly on flugelhorns and old or low-budget trumpets.

TIP

Monel or stainless steel

Most instruments have pistons made of monel, an alloy that slides well and doesn't wear easily. More expensive instruments may come with stainless steel pistons, for instance, which are said to be very durable. This material is also highly resistant to corrosion, and it slides very easily, typically requiring less frequent lubrication. If the alloy isn't specified, it's usually a student instrument that features a less expensive type of metal.

Piston guide

Piston guides, also known as *valve guides*, make sure that the piston's ports always align with the tubing, to prevent them from rotating in their casings. There are one- and two-point, metal and non-metal piston guides. You may come across every possible variation in most price ranges.

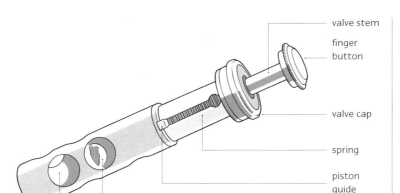

valve stem

finger button

valve cap

spring

piston guide

ports

A piston valve.

Smooth

When checking out an instrument, try the pistons for smooth, silent, and quick action. Of course they should be lubricated to function properly. If you depress a valve and then slide your finger off of the finger button, it shouldn't rattle or rebound.

Breaking them in

Often, the pistons start to slide as smoothly as they should only once the instrument has been played for a while: They need to be 'broken in'.

Springs

Naturally, not all valve springs are the same. If springs feel too stiff or too light, you can have them replaced quite cheaply. Some players reduce the springiness of their springs by making them shorter. Buying shorter or less springy springs instead allows you to switch back to the original springs.

Selecting finger buttons

Finger buttons come in different weights and shapes. Some players prefer concave buttons, for instance, while others prefer a convex shape. (Some trumpets come with two sets, one concave, the other convex.) If you're looking for a lighter, quicker action, you may get a set of light-weight finger buttons. Want something special? There are finger buttons with precious gem inlays too, and finger buttons with plastic inlays can be replaced by buttons that use mother-of-pearl. Do note that the use of (semi-)precious stones rather than plastic or mother-of-pearl may influence the tone of the instrument. Heavier stones are said to promote a more vibrant tone, for example.

Vented valves

If you move your first and third valve slides with the relevant pistons in the up position, you will feel a little pressure. *Vented valves* eliminate this pressure, allowing you to freely move the slides before or after playing the note you need them for. Some players like this; others don't. Because pressure doesn't build up, vented valves also eliminate the characteristic 'pop' sound when removing a valve slide with the relevant piston in the up position. Only few companies offer this type of valve — which seals and plays the way regular valves do — as an option.

TROMBONES

Trombones are different from trumpets because they have a slide, for one thing. Some have one or two valves too, but these are different from trumpet valves. First, a closer look at the slide of the instrument.

Stockings

If you take a close look at the ends of the inner slide of a trombone, you'll see a small bulge on either tube. The outer slide moves over these *stockings* rather than sliding over the entire surface of the inner slide. This makes things go a lot smoother.

Materials

The inner slide is often made of a different material than the outer slide: nickel silver on the inside, brass on the outside, for instance. This improves slide action and prevents corrosion. More expensive instruments may feature seamless tubing to make slide action even easier.

Light-weight slide

On some trombones you can opt for a *light-weight slide*. This will make the instrument 'feel' a little lighter and respond a little more easily. Likewise, various makers market a *narrow slide*, which is a little lighter to play.

Different slide

If a trombone sounds good but doesn't slide smoothly, try replacing the slide with one from an identical instrument.

Barrels

The *receiver barrels*, into which the hand slide falls, have a cork washer or a spring inside. Spring-loaded barrels allow you to pull the slide toward you a little further in the first position, and some trombonists use that difference to make certain notes sound a little higher.

Curve

The slight curve halfway along the gooseneck makes the slide point downwards a little. This improves the balance of the instrument.

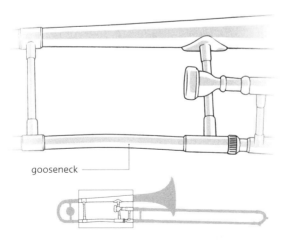

gooseneck

Most goosenecks have a slight curve.

Junior trombone

There are also trombones with a much larger arching in the

gooseneck. This makes it fit more comfortably around your neck, and it slightly reduces the overall length of the instrument. The first trombone of this kind, designed especially with children in mind, also has a shorter slide than a regular trombone, as well as a special pistol grip and an adjustable thumb rest.

Junior trombone with an arched gooseneck, a short slide and a pistol grip (Jupiter).

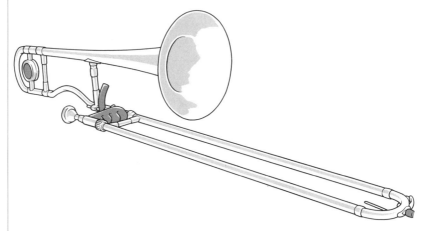

Ring
A simple solution for smaller hands is a ring on the inner slide brace. You put your first finger through the ring, instead of resting it against the mouthpiece or the receiver.

F-attachment
A trombone plays an octave lower than a trumpet, basically. There are trombones that can go a little lower still, with an extra piece of tubing and a valve. With this extra length, the B♭ in the

A rotary valve.

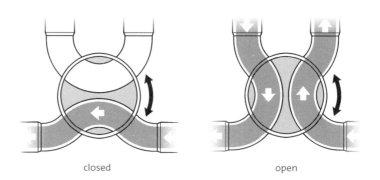

closed   open

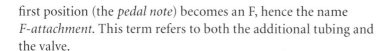
first position (the *pedal note*) becomes an F, hence the name *F-attachment*. This term refers to both the additional tubing and the valve.

Rotary valve

The valve of the F-attachment is a *rotary valve*, which is slightly more complicated than a piston valve. Rotary valves are also known as *rotors* or *cylinder valves*. (Note that there are trumpets with this type of valve as well; see page 139.)

Other positions

An F-attachment not only allows you to play lower notes: You can also play many of the 'original' notes in new positions. This makes certain trills and phrases easier to play, for instance.

Price

The price difference between a trombone without and with an F-attachment can easily vary from one to four hundred dollars, depending — among other things — on the price and the brand of the instrument.

Open or traditional

The extra tubing that goes with an F-attachment can either stick

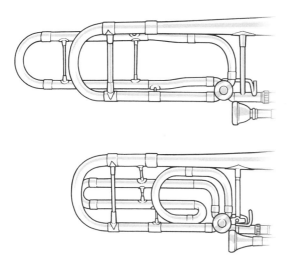

Open wrap.

Traditional wrap or closed wrap.

63

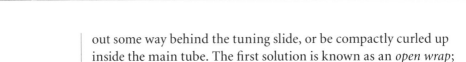

out some way behind the tuning slide, or be compactly curled up inside the main tube. The first solution is known as an *open wrap*; the second is called a *traditional* or *closed wrap*.

Free blowing but vulnerable

An open wrap avoids sharp bends in the tubing. This makes for a freer blowing instrument, and it reduces the difference between playing with the F-attachment or 'open' (i.e., without the F-attachment). On the other hand, an open wrap is more vulnerable, as the tubing sticks out. There are all kinds of in-between wrap designs as well.

TIP

> ### Convertible trombones
> On a convertible trombone you can take the whole F-attachment (F-section, F-wrap) off if you don't need it.

Straight trombones

Trombones without an F-attachment are referred to as *straight trombones*. To some, this is the true form of the instrument. Others feel that every trombone is a true trombone, no matter if it has valves or not.

BASS TROMBONES

A bass trombone is basically the same size as a tenor trombone, but it has a larger bore and bell, which makes the very lowest notes easier to play. Another difference is that nearly all bass trombones have two valves. The second valve adds yet another piece of tubing to the instrument.

Timbre

The main difference between a tenor and a bass trombone, however, is in the timbre of the instruments, not in the presence of any number of valves.

64

In-line or offset

On most older bass trombones, you can't use the second valve without the first one. This system is known as *stacked* or *offset*. The newer *in-line* or *independent* system, developed in the late 1960s, allows you to use both valves independently.

Not the same

That second rotor doesn't do the same thing on all bass trombones. It usually puts the instrument in the key of G♭ or G. Using both valves or rotors will then allow you to play low E♭ or D respectively.

Interchangeable tubing

Some bass trombones have interchangeable tubes for the second rotor, so that you can adapt its effect to the key you play in, for instance.

VALVES AND ROTORS

There are two basic types of trombone valve linkages. *Mechanical* or *ball-and-socket linkages* use metal parts only. The other type uses a nylon string, with names like *string rotor action*, *string action*, or *string F-valve linkage*.

Strings

A string linkage is less expensive and more likely to be noiseless. It also has a shorter lever stroke, and it's fairly easy to adjust yourself. On the other hand, strings can break or come loose.

Feel

A good, properly adjusted mechanism with a mechanical linkage is more expensive, and can be just as quiet. Of course, if one trombonist says a string 'feels' better, the next will disagree. Depending on the make of the instrument, you may be able to choose between string or metal. Conversion kits (mechanical to string) are also available.

65

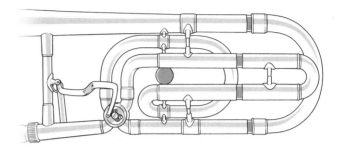

An F-attachment with string action (see page 125 for the string).

TIP

Testing

If you are play-testing a trombone with rotary valves, feel how smoothly the rotors work, listen to make sure they don't rattle when you let go of the lever, check the lever stroke and see if it's adjustable, and compare how the trombone plays with and without rotors. Using the rotor(s) usually increases the blowing resistance of the instrument, and the tone may be slightly altered. The exact effect may vary from one instrument to the other.

With or without rotors

A trombone usually plays differently as soon as you use the rotor: After all, it adds both a fair length of tubing and some tight bends to the instrument.

New designs

In order to reduce this difference, all kinds of new valves have been devised. Most companies now use so-called axial valves or axial flow valves, a design that minimizes the influence of the valve, making the instrument play more or less like a straight tenor trombones. When it comes to new valve designs, you will come across names such as Thayer, Hagmann, and Rotax (Willson). Some trombone makers sell their instruments with a choice of a new type of valve or a traditional rotor. Retrofitting your instrument with a modern type of valve is a costly affair.

VALVE TROMBONE

A *valve trombone* or *valved trombone* is something quite different again. The instrument has no slide, but it uses the same piston valves as a regular trumpet. Most brass instrument makers offer no more than a single model.

Jazz players

The valve trombone or valved trombone is mainly used in jazz, which explains the alternative term *jazz trombone*. It is often played by trumpeters who want to master the trombone as well, or who want to switch to that instrument. After all, the fingering is identical, and you don't need to get used to operating a slide.

Easier

Even without prior trumpet playing experience, most musicians feel that it's easier to learn how to play a valved trombone. It takes less time to learn to produce an acceptable sound or play a song, for example. Another advantage of the instrument is that the valves make fast, technical phrases easier to play.

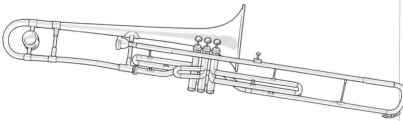

A valve trombone with three piston valves, and no slide.

A different sound

So why do most trombonists prefer the slide trombone? Because — according to those players — it sounds richer, more open and pure, because it has better intonation, because it allows you to play glissandos, and because of its mechanic advantages (the slide is less complicated than a set of valves). Also, valved trombones are not allowed in (most) contests.

Valved trombones vs. bass trumpets

The valved trombone (like the standard trombone) has roughly

67

the same range as a bass trumpet (see page 138), sounding an octave lower than a trumpet. Compared to the bass trumpet, a valved trombone typically sounds a bit mellower or smoother.

IN TUNE

On every wind instrument, there are notes that tend to sound sharp or flat. On trumpets, cornets, and flugelhorns, for example, you will need to adjust most of the notes that you play with both the first and third valve slide (e.g., D4 and G4 tend to be sharp; F5 tends to be flat). You can adjust these notes with the adjustable valve slides or kick slides, with your embouchure, or both.

Intonation
Usually, the better an instrument, the less you have to adjust the pitches of these notes: Better instruments usually have better *intonation*.

TIP

> ### Another horn
> *Brasswind makers all have their own ideas on how to improve the intonation of their instruments. As a result, every horn has its own deviations. If you are used to having to adjust a certain note on your horn, and you do the same on an instrument that has better intonation, that note may suddenly sound off — because you are overcompensating. In other words: You'll often need to get used to playing another horn, especially if it has a different intonation.*

Tests
There are a few tests that you can do to judge the intonation of an instrument, assuming you know how to play. If you can hear pitch deviations even without using the valves, it's probably better to put the horn away. Next, play all the notes you can get with the first

valve, then with the second, and so on. Another test: Play the scale of B, as this contains quite a lot of potential off-notes.

Trombone

Of course, a trombone is different, as the hand slide allows you to fine-tune every single note. So is there such a thing as an out-of-tune trombone? Yes: A trombone has bad intonation if the positions are too far from where they should be. When trying out a trombone pay special attention to middle and high F, middle D and high B♭, which can be flat. High notes are more likely to be out of tune than low ones, and you're more likely to hear that they are out of tune too.

A GOOD SOUND

An instrument not only needs good intonation, it also needs to have a good sound, whatever 'good' means in this context. If you don't yet play or you haven't been playing very long, you should ask a decent player to help you go through the following tips.

Somebody else

If you get somebody else to play a horn for you, it will never sound the same as when you play that instrument yourself. But as long as the same person demonstrates a number of horns for you, you will still be able to hear the differences between those instruments. Getting someone else to play also allows you to hear what they sound like at a distance — which is what your audience will hear.

TIP

> **Your mouthpiece**
>
> When choosing an instrument, always use your own mouthpiece (or an identical one) for all horns. If not, you won't be listening to the differences between the instruments you're playing, but to how you sound with one or more different mouthpieces.

69

The wall

As wind instruments direct the sound away from you, it's hard to get an idea of what your audience will hear. A tip: Play facing a wall, so the sound is reflected back to you. Trombonists can't use the slide if they stand to close to the wall. A solution? Put a book on a music stand and point the bell at the book.

Briefly at first

If you have to choose between a whole load of instruments, it's often best if you play only briefly on each one. Play something simple, so that you can concentrate on the instrument's tone, rather then on the notes you're playing.

Two by two

Once you have made a basic selection this way, start comparing these instruments two by two or three by three. Replace the one you like least with one from your basic selection. Compare. Replace the one you like least. And so on. Once you're about to make your final decision, you may want to play longer pieces so that you get to know the instruments better.

TIP

Mellow or bright

If you have no idea where to start when you walk into a store, ask the salesperson for two very different-sounding instruments. One with a very mellow character, and another that's known for its bright sound, for instance. Decide which sound you prefer and go on from there. Or compare a low-budget model with the most expensive instrument they have in stock, just to hear — and feel — how much they differ.

Response

An instrument must have a good response: Notes must speak easily and consistently. Try the response with loud and soft notes, from high to low. If you can hear even the softest notes at the back of the hall, the horn has good projection.

Loud or soft

An instrument doesn't just sound louder when you play harder; it sounds different too. More brilliant, edgy, or sizzling, ideally. That said, the difference should not be extreme. Some instruments may sound muddy, dull, or unclear when you play very softly or very low, or both, or they may sound very shrill, thin, or metallic when you play loud, high notes. When playing the entire range of the instrument, loud or soft, the changes should be very gradual, and even the loudest notes should not break up or distort.

Not the same

When two people listen to the same horn, they often use very different words to describe what they hear. What one considers shrill and thin (and so not attractive), another may consider bright or brilliant (and so not unattractive). And what one describes as dark and velvety, another may think dull or stuffy. It all depends on what you like, and on the words you use to describe it. What sounds good to you and what doesn't, largely depends on what you like to hear and on the type of music you play.

With and without

If you are trying out a trombone with an F-attachment, do all your play-testing both with and without it. Again, the almost unavoidable difference should be as small as possible.

Problem notes

Two potential problem notes on trombones are high A♭ and the highest D: They have a tendency to come out less than even.

Small differences

Even two 'identical' horns may sound slightly different, regardless of their price range. That means that you should always buy the very instrument that you auditioned, and not the 'same horn' from the stockroom. Of course, this is especially important if you're a good player. Most beginners will not be able to notice those — usually very subtle — differences.

71

PRE-OWNED INSTRUMENTS

There are lots of used instruments for sale, mainly because many players go on to buy a better horn after a few years. When you want to purchase a secondhand instrument, there are a few extra things to pay special attention to.

Your own mouthpiece
Take your own mouthpiece with you, if you have one. It's unlikely that you'll play comfortably with the mouthpiece that comes with the instrument.

Used mouthpieces
If you do buy a used mouthpiece, pay attention to the following:

- Most mouthpieces are silver-plated. If this **protective coating is damaged or worn out**, the brass below will make the mouthpiece taste bad.

- There's a chance of getting **a rash** too, as even the tiniest scratches can be home to even tinier bacteria.

- Some players aren't too bothered with a **pitted or scratched mouthpiece rim**: They like the extra bit of 'grip.'

- With or without scratches, always **clean** a used mouthpiece before trying it out (see pages 81 and 127–128).

- Mouthpieces that aren't too badly damaged can be **replated**. Expect to pay some twenty to thirty dollars.

The lacquer
Used instruments may have patches where the lacquer has disappeared, typically on spots where you touch the instrument as you play. These patches are very likely to make your hands smell of brass. Where there are scratches, even tiny ones, the lacquer can peel off, causing corrosion. Instruments can be relacquered or replated (see page 131).

The leadpipe
Remove the mouthpiece and the tuning slide to take a look

through the leadpipe, which should be clean and perfectly smooth inside. On a flugelhorn, do the same with the tuning mouthpipe. On a trombone you can look through the first slide tube if you take the outer slide off. A really dirty leadpipe can only be cleaned in a special bath (see page 131).

Spots

Small round patches on the leadpipe may indicate that it's corroding from the inside out. Replacing a trumpet's leadpipe can easily cost a hundred dollars or more.

Dents

Dents — even small ones — can affect the instrument's intonation. The closer a dent is to the mouthpiece, the sooner it will be a problem.

TIP

Appraisals

Lumps of solder can be a sign of sloppy repairs. You may also come across instruments that have had parts replaced, such as a leadpipe or a bell. If you don't want to take any risks, have the instrument appraised (see page 34–35) before buying it.

Valves

While one player presses the valves straight down, another may push them a little to the side, making them wear slightly more in that direction. If your way of playing is very different from the previous owner's, the valves may feel different to you than they ever did to him or her. Stiffer, for example.

Play

If you remove the valve caps and pull out the pistons a little, you shouldn't be able to move them sideways. If you can, they will probably leak. Getting valves repaired or replaced isn't cheap.

Pop

Check the instrument for leaky valves. Pull out the valve slides one by one, without pressing down the valves. Every slide should

produce an audible 'pop' sound when it comes off. If it doesn't, there's a leak (unless you're playing an instrument with vented valves; see page 60) in either the valve or the slide. The second valve slide especially can suffer from acidic perspiration, which may even produce tiny holes in the metal. If you have trouble getting the valve slides off, try using a cloth (see page 131).

Water key

If you don't get a 'pop' from the third valve slide, the problem may be the water key, which is easy to repair or replace. To check the water key you simply take the third slide off, close one end with your finger, and blow down the other end.

With one finger

Another leak test for the valves: Pull out the first tuning slide, depress the first valve, and blow through the instrument. If you put a finger on the tube the air is now coming from, there should be no leakage. Test the other valves in the same way.

Rotary valves

You can use this test for rotary valves too. Also feel how smoothly the rotor works, and check for excessive play. A tip: Opening and reassembling rotary valves requires experience and the right tools.

TIP

Rattles

Listen for rattles when playing the instrument. Also try the valves or rotors without playing. Unwanted noises can be the result of backlash, worn out felts, loose finger buttons, and broken springs, for example.

Checking the hand slide

Obviously, a trombone's slide should slide smoothly without leaking air. First check the water key. Take off the outer slide, close one end with a fingertip, and blow down the other. If that's okay, reassemble the slide, and rest its bend on the nose of your shoe. Close off both ends of the slide with your thumbs and quickly pull the inner slide upwards about ten or fifteen inches. If the outer

74

slide doesn't come along right away, something is leaking. You can also hold the slide in the air, close off the inner slide, and then let go of the outer slide. If it falls straight-away, it leaks. To avoid damage, you should of course make sure that the slide lands on a pillow or another soft surface. The first method is safer.

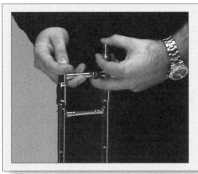

Tipcode TRP-008
This Tipcode shows you how you can check your trombone slide for leaks.

TIPCODE

No slide lock

Slide locks are a fairly new addition to the instrument. If you are looking at an old instrument, check to see if it has one. If it does, try it out. Some slide locks are so smooth that they open by themselves.

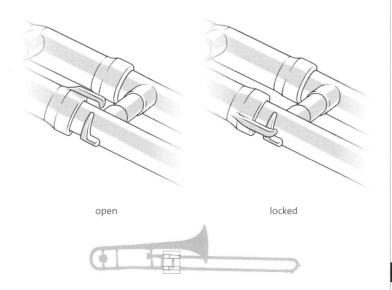

open   locked

A slide safety catch. Not all older trombones have one.

75

Serial numbers and bore

To determine the age of a horn, you need to know its serial number. You'll usually find it on one of the valve casings or on the bell. Lists of serial numbers and the corresponding years of manufacture of many brands can be found online (see page 201), and in some brasswind stores. A few brands also put the bore size on the valve casings.

6

Mouthpieces

The mouthpiece you use should fit you properly, like a pair of shoes, and it should fit your horn too. A chapter about everything you need to know to find the best one for your needs.

A mouthpiece that really suits you will allow you to get the tone you want with as little effort as possible. It'll make it easier to learn to play, to produce high and low notes, and to play in tune. It will also allow you to play for longer at a stretch.

Fit
A mouthpiece must suit your style of playing, as well as your embouchure and everything that goes with it, from the size and tension of your lips to your lung capacity, and the position of your teeth and jaws.

How it works
When you play, the rim of the mouthpiece rests against your lips. Your lips vibrate in the cup, and you blow the vibrating air into the instrument.

Main dimensions
Mouthpieces come in countless sizes and variations. The main 'parts' that determine how a mouthpiece will play and feel are:

- The **bore** or **throat**: the smallest opening of the mouthpiece.

- The **rim contour**: the width and shape of the edge or rim of the mouthpiece.

- The **diameter** and **depth** of the cup.

- The **backbore**: the shape of the inside of the shank.

Medium
Many players start out on a 'medium' mouthpiece, i.e., one with a

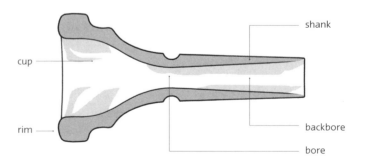

78

medium-sized rim, cup and bore. Most instruments are also sold with such mouthpieces. Of course, they are not necessarily the best solution for everybody.

- If you have rather soft, thick lips, a medium-sized rim is **too narrow** (it pinches), while it may be **too wide** for other lips, getting in their way.

- The cup may be **too small** for you (so you don't get a good sound) or **too big** (so that you have to work too hard).

- The bore can also be **too small** (which gives a poor response), or **too big** (making it hard to play in tune).

And those are just a few examples!

Small mouthpieces
Student instruments often come with small mouthpieces, because these are easier to play. One of the drawbacks? It's hard to develop a good embouchure with a mouthpiece that's too small.

Swapping or buying
When buying an instrument, most stores allow you to exchange the mouthpiece that comes with it. Good, pro-quality mouthpiece prices start around thirty or forty dollars, while top-of-the line models sell for over a hundred or two hundred dollars.

Fitting
A mouthpiece has all kinds of different dimensions, and as a player you have quite a few yourself too. Obviously, there's no simple rule to determine which mouthpiece suits you best. Reading this

Your own mouthpiece
If you go out shopping for a new mouthpiece, always bring the one you're currently playing. Based on its dimensions and your requirements (a bigger tone, easier high notes, a darker sound, or whatever) a good salesperson will be able to limit the number of mouthpieces to choose from to a handful, rather than you having to try out dozens.

TIP

79

chapter will help, and so can your teacher or a good — and patient
— salesperson.

Sound
A mouthpiece is not only important to how you play but also,
of course, to your sound. Classical players often select a 'large'
mouthpiece, which produces a warm, big tone that blends well
with the sound of the other instruments. If you play Latin or jazz,
for instance, you may be better off with a 'small' mouthpiece with
a shallow cup and a smaller bore, which gives you a crisper, more
brilliant sound. A tip: The largest mouthpieces require a good
player. The smallest ones do too.

Hundredths of an inch
When it comes to mouthpieces, hundredths of an inch count:
Even the smallest difference can makes for a big change in a
mouthpiece's playability. So when you go to buy a new mouthpiece
it's best not to choose one that is a lot bigger or smaller than the
one you are used to. A very different mouthpiece may seem great
when you buy it, but the chances are you won't stick with it.

*A trombone
mouthpiece
(above) is a
lot bigger.*

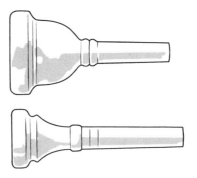

Testing tips
The easiest way to select a mouthpiece is to compare no more
than two or three at a time, just like when you're auditioning
instruments (see page 70). Try three models, choose the one that
feels best, replace the one you like least with another, and so on.
Note that you won't get used to a new mouthpiece as easily as you
would to a new instrument. Everything will feel different at first
and you'll need some time to adapt your embouchure.

TIP

Disinfectant

If you are choosing mouthpieces together with a fellow horn player, you will minimize the risk of a rashes and other symptoms if you thoroughly clean the mouthpieces before swapping them. Special mouthpiece disinfectants are available. If one of you has a cold sore, don't exchange mouthpieces at all.

Fits the trumpet

Most trumpet mouthpieces physically fit most trumpets without a problem, but not all. A fairly long mouthpiece with a fairly thin shank may sometimes slide in so far that it touches the inner edge of the leadpipe. As a result, the mouthpiece won't fit snugly, and air may even leak out. If a mouthpiece won't go in far enough, your tone may suffer from the distance between the shank and the leadpipe edge.

Cornet mouthpieces

Cornet mouthpieces come in two lengths. American (long) cornets usually require the long type, of course, and vice versa.

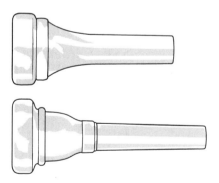

A long and a short cornet mouthpiece.

Flugelhorn mouthpieces

Flugelhorn mouthpieces don't always fit either. For example, those with a fairly narrow shank are often too thin for American-made flugelhorns. Sometimes this can be solved with a special adapter. If not, you'll have to find another mouthpiece.

81

Trombone mouthpieces

Trombone mouthpieces are available with a *large shank* for large-bore instruments and with a *small shank* for the smaller sizes.

THE DIFFERENCES

What exactly are the differences between deep and shallow cups, large and small bores or narrow, wide, rounded, and flat rims? What will gold-plating do for a mouthpiece and what difference does the weight of a mouthpiece make? These and many more questions are answered in the next sections.

Tricky

Mouthpieces come in hundreds of types and sizes. The fact that just about every manufacturer has its own system to identify the different models doesn't make life any easier. For instance, the Vincent Bach 7C, the Schilke 13B, and the Yamaha 11C4 are three trumpet mouthpieces with roughly the same dimensions, but very different names. Similarly, two 5A-mouthpieces by different makers may be nothing like each other.

Diameter and depth

The only thing that those model codes have in common is that the first figure tells you something about the cup diameter, while the letter that follows refers to the cup depth.

Help?

Does that help much? Not really: With one brand, a higher number means a larger diameter, while another company uses higher numbers for smaller sizes. Likewise, the letter A can indicate either a deep cup or a shallow one, depending on the mouthpiece make you're looking at.

More

Some mouthpieces have a longer code. An example would be a 12A4a: The second figure (4) refers to the shape of the rim (usually between 1 and 5, from very round to almost flat); the last letter refers to the backbore. This will often be between 'a' and 'e', from narrow to wide.

Comparable types

Fortunately, however, mouthpiece catalogs and websites on the subject often list 'similar' models made by other companies. They typically also list the diameter and depth of the cup, and the shape and width of the rim. Interested? Then check the web for a 'mouthpiece comparator' or a 'mouthpiece comparison chart'. Do add the type of instrument that you play (e.g., trumpet, trombone, or cornet, as there are similar charts for saxophone and clarinet mouthpieces!)

Descriptions

Many mouthpiece makers also describe the sound characteristics of each of their models — but note that depicting mouthpiece characteristics is as hard and subjective as putting flavors into words. Also, these descriptions tend to highlight the positive characteristics ('Makes high notes so much easier …'), while leaving out the negative ones ('… but low notes will be harder to play').

The same?

If you play both trumpet and flugelhorn, for instance, you may have noticed that some brands use the same codes for their trumpet and flugelhorn mouthpieces. However, that doesn't guarantee that they're similar mouthpieces. In other words: If you're perfectly happy with a 5A of a particular brand on your trumpet, their flugelhorn-5A is not necessarily your best choice.

The whole thing

In mouthpieces, all dimensions are interrelated. For instance, you will not come across mouthpieces with huge cups and very small bores, or the other way around. Even so, two mouthpieces with the same cup and bore dimensions may have slightly different characteristics: one of them may have a much wider backbore, for instance.

Wider cup, no air

Because everything is connected with everything else, and also

83

with how you play, it's not always easy to find what you're looking for. One more example? If you want a more powerful, bigger sound, you will need a wider cup. But if the bore that goes with it is too big for you, you can run out of air very quickly.

Sound, feel, and play

So each change in one thing affects everything else, in a mouth-piece. Still, to get a better idea of what mouthpieces are about, it's good to have a look at how various measurements influence the sound they're likely to produce, and the way they feel or play.

THE CUP

For trumpets and cornets, the cup diameter can vary from about 0.59" to 0.69" (15–17.5 mm). For a tenor trombone, add about 0.4". If letters are used to designate cup size, then 'C' usually indicates a medium cup.

Big

It takes a good player to handle a mouthpiece with a really big cup. Otherwise, it will be difficult to play in tune and to play large intervals (from high to low notes and the other way around), and you will quickly run out of breath.

Small

If the cup is too small for you, then your lips can't vibrate freely.

TIP

> ### The biggest you can handle
>
> *One thing that just about everyone agrees on is that you should choose the biggest cup diameter you can handle with your embouchure. This helps to increase your control, endurance, and tone quality. Larger cups also enhance your volume of sound, and they promote a fuller tone and a darker timbre.*

84

Your timbre will suffer, and you'll be more likely to miss notes. A small cup may make hitting the highest notes a little easier, though — but if it's too small, you can forget them altogether.

Cup size and pitch
Cup size influences the pitch of your instrument. A larger cup makes for a lower pitch, while a smaller cup brings the pitch up. In other words, cup size should also be matched to your instrument.

Same numbers, different sizes
The cup flares out a little at the top. The higher up you measure it, the bigger the cup diameter will appear. That's why two cups labeled 0.60" may actually have different sizes.

Thick lips
Some experts say that big lips require a big cup diameter, and vice versa. That seems pretty obvious. Still, lots of successful musicians have proven that it doesn't need to work that way. In other words, there are players with big lips that use small diameter cups, and the other way around.

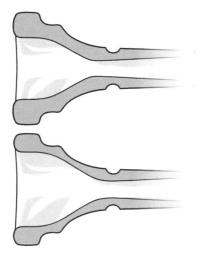

A deep, wide cup, and a smaller, shallower one.

Cup depth
Cups also differ in their depth. A deeper cup is harder work to play, but you may get a warmer, bigger, darker tone in return. A shallow cup, like a smaller one, is less tiresome to play, and gives

85

a brighter, edgier tone. High notes are easier to hit, but you may loose some tone in the lower registers, as well as a bit of volume. Mouthpieces with adjustable and replaceable cups (see pages 88 and 93) are available too.

Cup shape

The cup of trumpet, cornet, and trombone mouthpieces is basically U-shaped on the inside, while the cup of a flugelhorn mouthpiece is shaped much more like a V. The more a cup of any type of mouthpiece tends toward a V-shape, the warmer, mellower, and less bright or edgy the tone will be, and vice versa.

Two very similar cups on two very different mouthpieces.

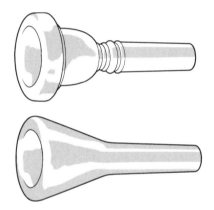

Cup 1, cup 2

Some companies refer to the *first cup* (the upper part of the cup) and the *second cup* (the lower part). For example, a mouthpiece with a relatively narrow first cup makes high notes easier, while the tone will stay nice and dark due to a rather wide second cup.

THE RIM

The rim, the part that you hold against your lips, is especially important for how a mouthpiece feels. The width is usually somewhere between 0.200" and 0.240" (5–6 mm). Again add about 0.04" for tenor trombones.

Wide or narrow

The wider the rim is, the more evenly its pressure will be distributed over your lips. In other words, a thicker rim is less tiresome to play. This explains why really wide, flat rims are referred to as *cushion rims*. Apart from a softer bite, such rims also promote a fuller sound. On the downside, a wide rim offers less control over the sound and the pitch, and high notes become harder to play. Do note that some companies used the term 'cushion rim' for a very specific rim design.

Narrower rim

If you need to take the instrument from your mouth to play large intervals (from really high to really low notes, or vice versa), you may want to try a mouthpiece with a narrower rim.

TIP

Round or flat

If you have thick, soft lips, you are more likely to need a wide rim with a rather flat contour. A narrow rim with a high-point, rounded contour can make both small and large intervals easier, and high notes will be easier to hit, possibly expanding your range. On the downside, it can pinch your lips and reduce your endurance.

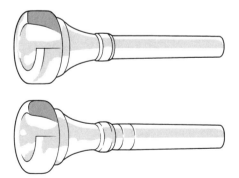

A fairly flat and a fairly rounded rim.

Rim bite

Even the shape of the inner edge (*rim bite*) makes a difference. A sharper rim bite increases the response and facilitates the attack,

87

but sliding from note to note may become harder, as does playing for a long time. A smooth rim bite is more comfortable, but attacking notes becomes harder, as does playing in tune, and air and saliva may escape while you play.

An easy mistake

Some mouthpieces feel bigger or smaller than they really are, because of the position of the highest point of the rim. If this point is toward the outside of the rim, it will make the mouthpiece feel bigger than it actually is, and vice versa.

The same rim

Most horn players who play more than one instrument (i.e., players who *double*) choose a mouthpiece with the same shape of rim for each horn. That makes switching instruments easier. If you can't find a mouthpiece with the rim you're looking for, there are specialists who can make or copy one for you.

Mouthpiece kits

Various companies make *mouthpieces kits* or *modular mouthpieces* with interchangeable cups and/or backbores, allowing you to change your sound without changing your rim.

Mouthpiece with inter-changeable cups.

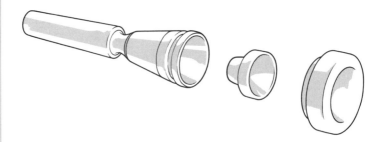

THE BORE

The bore or throat is the smallest opening of the mouthpiece. It must be big enough to let the air pass through, while being small enough to provide sufficient resistance.

88

Large or small

Other than that, the influence of the bore is similar to what bore sizes elsewhere on the instrument do.

- If you want a flexible, free-blowing instrument, lots of volume, and easy low notes, go for a **large bore** — but you'll need more air and a well-developed embouchure.

- A **smaller bore** or throat makes for a brighter sound. It increases the playing resistance and enhances the response of the instrument, and the high register becomes easier to play.

If the bore gets too small, however, the mouthpiece may seem to 'shut off' when you try to play the highest notes.

A mouthpiece with a large bore and a wide rim, and one with a small bore and a narrow rim; the opposite combination is equally possible.

THE BACKBORE

Backbores can have various designs, from V-shaped to barrel-shaped. By far the majority are V-shaped. If you have a lot of air, you may benefit from a barrel-shaped backbore. The opposite design (though it's very rare) may be a solution if you have very little air.

Bigger, smaller

Apart from variations in shape, the backbore influences the sound in a similar way to the bore. The 'narrower' it is, the brighter the sound. A very small backbore, however, can make for a stuffy high register. The 'wider' it is, the darker and mellower the sound. This explains why an open backbore is often referred to as a symphonic backbore. If it's too wide or too large, however, the mouthpiece will lack resistance.

89

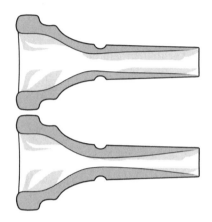

An open, slightly barrel-shaped backbore, and a narrow, V-shaped backbore.

Pitch and volume

Backbore size and shape can also affect pitch and the volume of sound of the instrument. Some companies offer their mouthpieces with a choice of different backbores. Other have special backbore designs, such as a stepped backbore.

WEIGHT

All kinds of benefits are attributed to heavier mouthpieces. That is why several companies market mouthpieces in two versions: an regular model next to a weighted version. The latter usually cost a little more, and they often come with descriptive names like Mega Tone (Bach) or Heavytop (Denis Wick).

A standard cornet mouthpiece (short model) and a weighted version.

Boosters

Rather than buying a weighted mouthpiece, you can get a *mouthpiece booster*. Some boosters look like large, separate cups, which you push onto the mouthpiece; others look like nothing more than a set of metal rings.

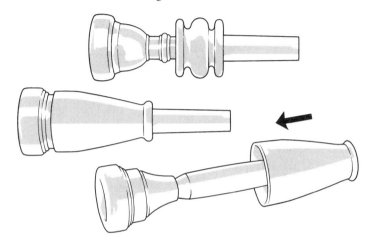

Various mouthpiece boosters.

The same

The extra weight in a mouthpiece may help you produce anything from an intensified, more stable tone with a solid core, to less distortion when playing really loudly, and from a darker tone to more accuracy in the higher register. Also, it may increase your control over the entire range of the instrument. On the other hand, a non-weighted mouthpiece enhances the response of your instrument and makes it easier to control and color the tone.

MATERIALS

Most mouthpieces are made of silver-plated brass, but there are other materials to choose from.

Silver or gold

Brass leaves an unpleasant taste and can cause a rash, so the silver-plating is no mere luxury. If your skin or your lips can't cope

91

with silver, or if you make silver tarnish quickly, a gold-plated mouthpiece may be the solution. They're expensive, though, and gold plating won't last as long as silver plating.

Solid silver and aluminum

Rather than a weighted, silver-plated mouthpiece, you could go for a solid silver one. The sheer weight of this metal will give you a stronger, darker sound. At the opposite end of the scale are ultra-light aluminum mouthpieces that respond very easily and offer very bright high notes.

Plastic

For players who are allergic to all metals there are synthetic mouthpieces, or metal mouthpieces with a plastic rim. Some companies make pro-quality mouthpieces with a hard resin cup. Plastic mouthpieces are usually used by marching and school bands, and for hot or cold weather gigs. Low-cost plastic mouthpieces are available in a variety of bold colors.

Wood

Wooden mouthpieces, which are even rarer, promote a mellow tone. If you like this type of sound but don't like the feel of a wooden rim, metal mouthpieces with a wooden cup are also available.

AND FINALLY

You'll need to get used to a new mouthpiece, just as you would to a new pair of shoes. If you go straight ahead and play for hours with a new mouthpiece, you definitely risk sore lips. Another warning: It can take quite a while before you realize that your mouthpiece is causing problems. If you practice a lot but you aren't making any progress, it may not be only your mouthpiece — but it very well could be.

Fifty or one

There are professional horn players who still use the standard,

92

middle of the road mouthpiece their teacher gave them thirty years ago. There are others who have tried at least fifty different models and are still looking for the perfect one. There's a fair chance these players will never find it. There's also a good chance that the first category of horn player has an 'easy embouchure' and the second type doesn't. Or that the second type simply loves to experiment, or just to spend money on their horn. Tips on buying pre-owned mouthpieces are on page 72.

Brands

Vincent Bach, Burbank, Marcinkiewicz (MMP), Schilke, and Yamaha are some well-known mouthpiece manufacturers that also make instruments. Other instrument makers also have their own mouthpieces, which they don't necessarily design or produce themselves. Then there are brands that supply only mouthpieces, and sometimes other brasswind products as well. Greg Black, Bush, Curry, Giardinelli, Faxx, Josef Klier, Laskey, Jet-Tone, Bob Reeves, Stork, Warburton, and Denis Wick are some well-known examples. Some companies that supply special mouthpieces are Jerwyn (adjustable cup depth), Asymmetric (asymmetric cup to enhance the high range), Loud (increases your volume), Parduba (double cup design, combining two cup shapes in one mouthpiece), Rudy Muck, and Zottola.

7

Mutes

The only mutes that really mute, so that the sound is muffled almost completely, are the practice mutes discussed in Chapter 3. All other types of mutes are mainly used to create special effects, and timbres that range from razor-sharp to velvety-soft.

Most types of mutes are hollow cones in various sizes and shapes. They're held in place in the bell by a few strips or a ring of cork. The three best-known types are the *straight mute*, the *cup mute*, and the *harmon mute*. The exact effect of each of these types can differ from brand to brand, of course.

Straight mute

The most commonly used type is the straight mute. If a classical piece specifies that you should play *con sordino* (with mute), you will be required to use this model. It largely closes off the bell, making your instrument sound a little like talking while holding your nose, i.e., slightly nasal and a bit thin or shrill.

TIPCODE

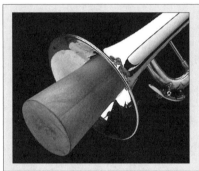

Tipcode TRP-009
This is how straight mutes influence the trumpet sound.

Cup mute

The cup mute looks like a straight mute with a cup. The inside of the cup is often finished with thin, soft material that slightly muffles the sound. Some models have an adjustable cup. The

TIPCODE

Tipcode TRP-010
The Tipcode demonstrates the effect of an adjustable cup mute, both open and closed.

96

closer it is to the bell, the more it mutes the sound and the 'smaller' the sound becomes. Some cup mutes can double as practice mutes: See if you can move the cup right up against the bell.

Harmon, wah-wah, wow, bubble

The third popular type of mute comes with a host of different names, from harmon mute to *wow, wow-wow* or *wah-wah mute, bubble mute, extending tube,* or *E.T. mute.* It has a cork ring that closes off the bell entirely, the sound coming out of a hole in the mute only. As with the straight mute, the effect is often called 'nasal', but it is very different. A little more metallic, you could say.

Tipcode TRP-011
In Tipcode TRP-011 you can hear the effect of a harmon mute.

TIPCODE

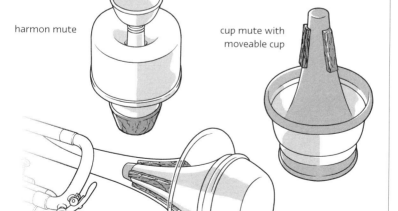

stem

harmon mute

cup mute with moveable cup

straight mute

The three most popular types of mutes.

97

Laurel & Hardy

Harmon mutes virtually always come with a small adjustable pipe that you can stick into the mute. Opening and closing this stem with your hand creates the 'bubble' trumpet noises often used in old slapstick movies, for example.

Aluminum, wood or plastic

Most mutes are made of aluminum, producing a brighter, edgier sound than wood or fiberboard mutes. Some aluminum mutes have copper or brass bottoms that make for a more powerful or fuller sound. The sound of a plastic mute is usually somewhere between metal and wood. Plastic models are usually less expensive and more resilient than aluminum ones. You may occasionally see mutes made entirely of steel, copper, or another metal. These are typically both heavier and more expensive.

Prices

Mutes typically cost between some fifteen and fifty dollars. The most affordable ones are usually made of fiberboard or plastic; the most expensive mutes are usually special aluminum models, say with a copper bottom. Trombone mutes always cost a little more.

Plunger

There are many other types of mutes. The *plunger*, for example, is so called simply because it looks like one. This type of mute is used for *doo-wah* effects. At the 'doo' you smother the sound by closing the bell, and at the 'wah' you take the mute off. Some players use hats, known as *Derby mutes*, instead of rubber or metal plungers.

TIPCODE

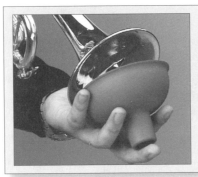

Tipcode TRP-012
This Tipcode briefly demonstrates are some characteristic plunger effects.

A plunger.

A plunger.

Bucket mute

As you would expect, a *bucket mute* is a small bucket that is usually attached to the bell with three small clamps. It's filled with a soft material such as mineral (rock) wool or foam plastic, which makes for a soft, smooth tone. That's why bucket mutes often have the word 'velvet' in their names. If you want a flugelhorn-like sound on a trumpet, you can do worse than try a bucket mute. This type

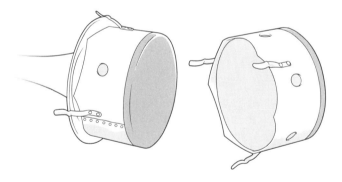

Bucket mute or velvet mute.

Many more mutes

There are many more types of mutes, including foldable and washable neoprene mutes that fit over your bell, or even over another mute. Lots of mutes come with very descriptive names, from the clear-tone mute, which looks like two straight mutes fitted together, to the sweet sounding mel-o-wah, the buzzing wee-zee, the penetrating megaphone, and the whispering whispa-mute, for example.

TIP

99

of mute is available in various depths. The deeper it is, the more pronounced the effect will be.

MORE ON MUTES

A mute not only makes your instrument sound different, it makes it play differently too. You have to work harder, your volume goes down and the pitch often goes up a little. You'll notice this most with the lower notes. If they become sharp because of the mute, just pull your tuning slide out a little. The degree in which you need to fine-tune notes, and the increase in blowing resistance depend on the design and the material of the mute. Badly-designed mutes can make it very hard to play in tune.

Moisten the cork
A mute must fit into or around the bell of your instrument properly. If it won't stay in place, don't use any force but instead moisten the cork strip(s). No tap handy? Saliva will do too.

Mute holder
There are various types of mute holders that can hold one, two, or more mutes, or even a drink. Most mute holders are designed to clamp to the tube or the music ledge of a music stand.

Brands
Some examples of companies that make mutes are Belmonte, Tom Crown, Humes & Berg, Jo-Ral, Denis Wick, Charles Davis, Harmon, Charlie Spivak, and Ullvén, the latter from Sweden. Most of them also make other accessories.

8

Tuning and Accessories

Before you start playing, you need to make sure that your valves or your slide are properly lubricated, and you'll have to tune your instrument. Taking a little care of your instrument when you stop playing may save you a lot of maintenance later. This chapter focuses on everything you do before and after playing, and also includes tips on cases, gig bags, instrument stands, lyres, amplifying your instrument, and tips for on the road.

If you really want to keep your instrument in good condition, you'll need to do some work on it at home too. This is covered in Chapter 9.

Out of the case
Preferably lift a trumpet, cornet, or flugelhorn out of its case by the valve casings.

Mouthpiece
Insert the mouthpiece into the leadpipe with a light twisting motion. Don't push or knock it in, as it may get stuck that way.

Assembling a trombone
Always grasp the bell section of a trombone by the bell stay. Then grab the slide by its inner and outer braces to prevent the outer slide from slipping off. Now hold the slide with the bow downwards and fit the bell into it with your other hand.

TIPCODE

Tipcode TRP-013
This short movie shows you how to assemble a trombone step by step.

Perpendicular
Make sure the bell section is exactly perpendicular to the slide,

TIP

Food and drinks
If you want to make it as easy as possible to keep your horn clean, wash your hands and brush and floss your teeth before you play, and don't drink anything that contains sugar when you're playing.

and only then — gently — tighten the bell lock nut. If you twist the bell into its perpendicular position after you've tightened the nut, you may not be able to get it loose again: By twisting the bell, even slightly, you soon apply more force than you think. Only fit the mouthpiece once you have assembled your trombone.

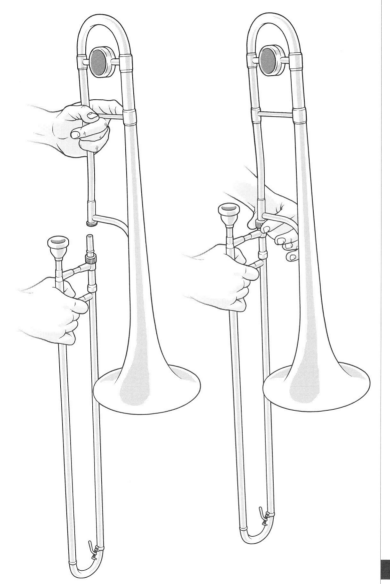

Fit the bell into the slide and — gently — tighten the bell lock nut.

VALVES AND SLIDES

Valves must always be lubricated using dedicated valve oil. In order to do the job properly, you need to take the pistons out. (See Chapter 9, which also covers the various lubricants.)

Upside down
If a piston valve gets a little slow, you are overdue in oiling it. A quick solution is to hold your instrument upside down and to drip a little valve oil into the holes of the bottom caps while moving the pistons. If you use too much oil, most of it will probably run straight out again.

Rotary valves
Oiling a rotary valve always takes more time, so you're better off doing it before the gig, and preferably at home (see page 124–125).

Trombone slides
Lubricating your trombone slide, too, is a job best done at home. Turn to page 127 to read how. Just before playing, use a special spray bottle to sprinkle some cool, clear tap water over the inner slide. This makes it move as smoothly as it can. There are all kinds of special agents that can be added to the water. Some trombonists are sure that they help, others prefer to do without. A tip: Always empty the spray bottle before you put it in your case.

TUNING

Tuning your instrument is very easy, basically: You simply move the tuning slide out until you get exactly the right pitch. The hard part of tuning, however, is to learn to hear when the pitch is right, and to play the required note without pitch fluctuations.

Too cold
If your instrument is very cold, it may sound flat, even with the

tuning slide pushed fully in. This means you'll have to warm it up. Do this by breathing soundlessly through it (as if you're using the water keys, but less vigorously), or simply by playing the instrument for a while. A cold mouthpiece feels uncomfortable: Keep it in your pocket or hold it in your hand to warm it up. If you have to play outside and it's cold, you may use a lip saver: a soft, thin cover that slides over your mouthpiece.

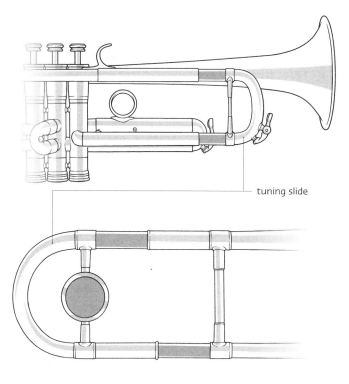

The extended tuning slide of a trumpet.

tuning slide

The extended tuning slide of a trombone.

Tuned to A

Many orchestras and bands tune to the A4, which is the A above Middle C (see page 19). If you play that note on a piano, the strings vibrate 440 times per second.

A=440

This pitch is indicated as A=440 hertz, 440Hz, or 440 vps (vibrations per second). Tipcode TRP-014 plays this pitch for you, allowing you to tune your instrument to it.

105

TIPCODE

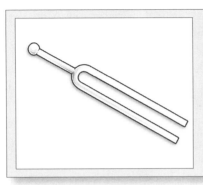

Tipcode TRP-014

This Tipcode plays the reference pitch A=440. You can repeat this Tipcode as often as you like while tuning your instrument.

Tuning fork

If you don't have a piano or the Tipbook website at hand, the most affordable way to get this reference pitch is using a tuning fork. Tap its prongs against your knee, set the stem against your ear or on a table, and you'll hear a concert A. (Tuning forks in other tunings are available as well.) Electronic metronomes can often play this pitch too.

TIPCODE

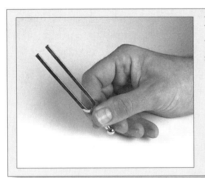

Tipcode TRP-015

The tuning fork in this Tipcode is tuned to A=440 as well.

Concert A or B♭

On a trumpet, a flugelhorn, or a cornet, you get a concert A by playing a B. Bands with lots of B♭ instruments may tune to concert pitch B♭. If so, you have to play a C.

Trombone

On a trombone you play the A with the slide in the second position. An F-attachment needs to be tuned separately. It has its own tuning slide.

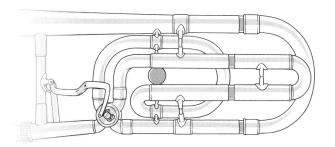

The F-attach-ment needs to be tuned separately.

How far?

Learning to tune your instrument takes time. First, you'll have to learn to hit the desired note (A or B♭) without pitch fluctuations. Second, you may have trouble hearing whether you're sharp (so you have to extend the tuning slide) or flat (so you have to push it in, raising the pitch).

Practice

A tip to practice hearing pitch differences: Play a note with the tuning slide fully extended (prevent it from slipping off!). Then push it all the way in and play the same note again. It will sound noticeably higher, maybe only after some practice. If you can clearly hear this pitch difference, reduce the distance you move the tuning slide, so the resulting difference will be smaller — and again try to hear what happens.

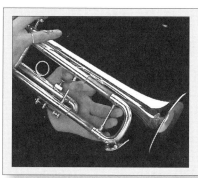

Tipcode TRP-016

If you start with a fully extended tuning slide, you will hear the pitch go up as you pull it in slowly.

TIPCODE

An inch

Another tip: To tune to A=440 on a trumpet, you probably don't

107

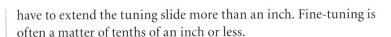
have to extend the tuning slide more than an inch. Fine-tuning is often a matter of tenths of an inch or less.

Tuners

You can also use an electronic tuner. This is a small device that shows you the pitch you play and whether it's sharp, flat, or in tune. Most tuners have a small microphone built in. As an alternative, there are clip-on tuners. You simply clip this device on the bell of your instrument. It will register the pitch you play without responding to the notes produced by your fellow band members. Tip: If you go out to buy a tuner, see if your model of choice has an auto power-off feature. This definitely helps save batteries.

Transposing tuners

Various electronic tuners can be adjusted to the key your instrument is in. Shift it to the appropriate key and it will display the note you're fingering, rather than the sounding note.

An automatic, chromatic electronic tuner. The A it hears, sounds a little flat.

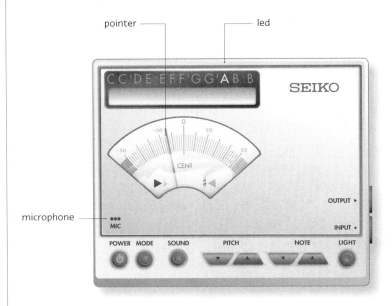

Weak

If you need to extend the tuning slide almost fully, for instance because you have to tune to a very low-pitched piano, you won't just get a lower pitch. Your sound will also become weak and

108

uncentered, and the intonation of your instrument will suffer: Notes may start to deviate more than usual.

New mouthpiece?

A new mouthpiece may require a different 'standard' position of your tuning slide, either because it slides further or less far into the receiver, or because it has a different bore, cup, or backbore size.

TIP

A little higher

Some orchestras tune just a little higher, for instance to A=442, for a slightly brighter sound. There are tuning forks that produce that pitch too, and electronic tuners can often be adjusted to different pitches.

TIPCODE

Tipcode TRP-017
The difference between A=440 and A=442 may not be that obvious at first. Playing the two pitches simultaneously clearly produces two 'beats' per second, caused by the 2Hz pitch difference.

AFTER PLAYING

It's easiest to keep a mouthpiece clean by simply rinsing it with lukewarm water after playing. If your case or gig bag doesn't have a mouthpiece holder, keep it in a leather or synthetic pouch. These sell for some five to fifteen dollars, usually featuring a zipper or a snap closure. Molded pouches are also available, as well as models that hold two or more mouthpieces.

109

Not on its rim
Always set your mouthpiece down on its side, never on its rim. This prevents scratches and dents, as long as it doesn't roll off the table.

Removing moisture
When you play, you'll use your water key to remove most of the moisture (condensation) that collects in your instrument. It's best to get rid of the rest of it when you're done playing. Remove the valve slides, and blow through the instrument as if you were using the water key(s). A tip: When pulling out a valve slide, first depress the corresponding valve to prevent excessive wear.

The dryer it is
The better you dry the parts of your instrument after playing, the less maintenance your horn will require and the longer it will last. Some horn players leave their cases open when they get home, so that everything can dry some more.

Tuning slide and valve caps
After playing, push your tuning slide in all the way. If you don't, it may get stuck in the long run. Likewise, some players always loosen their valve caps a bit after playing. This keeps them from getting stuck due to corroded screw threads.

Cloth
Sweat can damage lacquer, brass, and silver, so run a soft, lint-free cloth over your instrument after playing. Don't forget the inside of the bell. An old (unprinted) T-shirt or a dish cloth will do fine, and there are special brasswind cleaning cloths available too.

CASES AND BAGS

New instruments usually come with a basic rectangular case that features one or more holes to put your mouthpiece(s) in, and a separate pocket for valve oil and other accessories. A plush or velvet lining prevents scratches. If your instrument didn't come with a case, or if you want another one, here's what you can choose from.

More space

Good hard-shell cases usually have a strong plywood or molded plastic core. The rectangular models have more space than others. Larger cases even allow you to store one or more mutes, a music stand, and sheet music, and there are special cases designed to carry two or even three instruments. Double-wall cases offer extra protection. *Tip:* Some cases allow you to store the instrument with a mute in the bell!

Trombone cases

Trombone cases flare out at the bell. They should always match the instrument's bell size, which can vary quite a lot (see page 45).

Prices

Basic trumpet cases start at around fifty or seventy-five dollars, but you can easily go up to six times as much, or more. Shaped or contoured cases, usually with a hard plastic shell, may be just as strong, but they offer less space.

Gig bag

A *gig bag* is a thickly lined bag, often made of water-resistant synthetic cloth, and slightly shaped for the instrument. Gig bags often have one or more extra pockets, as well as shoulder or backpack straps. You can buy a decent one for around fifty dollars, but prices can go up to a hundred fifty or more for special designs (e.g., bags that hold two or three instruments) or materials, such

Locked

Most cases can be locked. More than anything, these small locks are there to prevent the lid from springing open if the case falls. A separate case cover (Cordura, canvas, leather) will do so too, as well as offering additional protection against rain and dirt.

111

A gig bag with a shoulder strap.

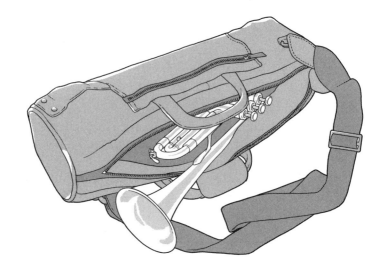

as leather. Most gig bags won't protect your instrument as well as a good case does, but gig bags are more comfortable to carry around.

Conceal the shape
If you don't want everyone to know that you have one or more instruments with you, you can also get carryall bags that conceal their shape — unless you happen to play the trombone.

Locks and hinges
Check to see how sturdy latches, locks, zips, hinges, and handles are. These parts tend to be the weak points on many cases and gig bags. Plastic clips and rings may not be as strong as metal ones.

And more
Some cases and bags also feature extras such as safety reflector strips, a sleeve to hide the shoulder straps, flush latches, a spring-return handle, or a waterproof 'rain coat'.

Too hot
Always store your instrument in its case or bag, rather than leaving it on a table or a chair. Never leave an instrument where it can get too hot: High temperatures can cause valves and valve slides to jam, and brass gets hotter than you might think in the sun.

Backpack

If you are transporting your case or bag in a backpack, always pack it so that the bell is pointing upwards.

INSTRUMENT STANDS

If you take a break, it's best to put your instrument in its case or bag, or else put it on a stand. Most trumpet stands are simple tripods with a wooden or plastic peg, over which you slide the bell of your instrument. For a flugelhorn you need one with a larger peg. The very smallest trumpet stand is designed so that you can store it in the bell of your horn when folded up.

Five or three

Most five-legged stands are less easily kicked over than the standard three-legged designs.

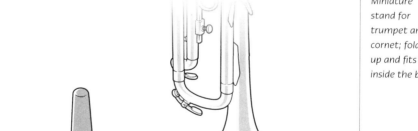

Miniature stand for trumpet and cornet; folds up and fits inside the bell.

113

Trombone stands

Trombone stands are larger, of course. When folded up, they're usually the size of a music stand. Stands mainly differ in how easily and small they fold up, in how sturdy they are, and in how much stability they offer.

No stand

If you don't use a stand, always put down a trumpet or cornet on its left side (seen from the player's point of view) to prevent damaging the vulnerable second valve slide.

LYRES

Marching musicians attach their (small, marching size) sheet music to their instrument with a *lyre*. Many horns have a lyre holder for that purpose. On some trumpets, you need to remove you third valve slide ring and insert your lyre holder instead. If you want to have a permanent holder and do not want to sacrifice the third valve slide ring, you can ask a brasswind technician to solder one onto your instrument. Don't try this at home!

The lyre replaces the third valve slide ring.

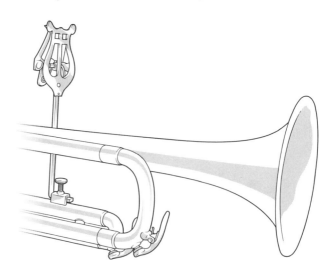

Clip-on
Alternatively, there are lyres that can simply be clicked onto the instrument.

Designs
There are all kinds of clever lyre designs, and special flip folder windows help prevent your music from getting wet. Lyres come in plastic and metal.

Lyre with click–on system for lyre holder.

AMPLIFYING YOUR INSTRUMENT

Brass winds are among the loudest wind instruments, but if you play it in a band with electric instruments and a drummer, you will soon need to be amplified.

Wind instrument microphones
Many microphone makers have special wind instrument microphones. These may not look very different from vocal microphones, but they are. Two examples:

• Instrument microphone are built to handle the **higher sound pressure level** (SPL) of a wind instrument — and brasswinds can generate high SPLs!

• Vocal microphones have a built-in **pop filter** that reduces

115

the 'explosions' you create when singing so-called plosive consonants (e.g., P, B, T). When used for a wind instrument, this filter tends to cancel out essential frequencies.

Pickup pattern

Microphones come with different *pickup patterns*, which refers to how they respond to sounds coming from different directions. For wind instruments, a microphone with a heart-shaped or cardioid pickup pattern, tends to be the best choice if you want to pick up the natural sound of the instrument. A microphone with a super cardioid pattern is less sensitive for feedback, but it produces a more direct, less natural sound.

Small membrane

Most wind instrument microphones are small-membrane condenser microphones. If you want to know what that means, please check out *Tipbook Amplifiers and Effects* (see page 224).

Stand-mounted microphones

Using a stand-mounted microphone limits your freedom of movement. If you move the instrument away from the microphone, the volume will decrease. Moving too close can make for a boomy sound due to the mic's *proximity effect*. You can use all of this to your advantage, increasing the dramatic effect and the dynamic range of the instrument, but it's often easier to use a dedicated instrument-mounted microphone.

TIP

Try them out

Just like instruments, microphones all have their own sound characteristics. Whether you buy a stand-mounted microphone or a clip-on system, always try out various models, preferably with your own instrument.

Pre-amp

Clip-on systems usually feature condenser microphones. The power that this type of microphone needs is usually supplied by a small, typically belt-worn preamplifier, which also allows you to adjust volume and other parameters.

Prices

Prices for these systems range from about three to five hundred dollars, but you may find systems that cost less. Wireless systems are more expensive.

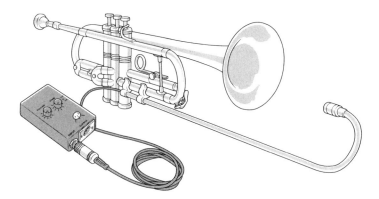

Trumpet microphone with clamp and preamplifier.

Effects

Brass players use far fewer electronic effects than electric guitarists do, but the use of a *reverb* and a *delay* is quite common. Other effects (e.g., *flangers*, *wah-wahs*, or a *chorus*) can be fun to experiment with.

Amps and effects

If you use a microphone more often than not, you may consider purchasing your own amp too, and possible some types of effects that help enhance your sound. More information on these products, and on microphones, cables, wireless systems and related subjects can be found in *Tipbook Amplifiers and Effects* (see page 224).

ON THE ROAD

When you travel with your instrument, which includes visits to your teacher, you may find the following tips helpful:

- **In the car**, your instrument is usually safest between the back and front seats. The worst place is under the rear window, especially on a sunny day.

- When using **public transportation**, keep your horn on your lap. It's safe, and you won't forget it this way.

- Flying out? Then take it along as **hand luggage**.

- If you still leave your horn behind somewhere, you're more likely to get it back if your **name, (email) address, and phone number** are listed inside your case or bag.

- Consider **insuring your instrument**. Musical instruments fall under the insurance category of 'valuables.' A regular homeowner insurance policy will usually not cover all possible damage, whether it occurs at home, on the road, in the studio, or onstage.

- To get your instrument insured you'll need to know the **serial number** (see page 76) and some other details, which you can list on pages 218–219 of this book. Insurance companies may also require an appraisal (see page 34–35) and proof of purchase.

9

Maintenance

If you want to keep your instrument in optimum playing condition and enjoy it as long as you can, you will need to clean it on a regular basis. Also, valves and slides need to be lubricated from time to time. Other than that, brass instruments require little maintenance. This chapter suggests what you can easily do yourself and what you should probably leave to a professional.

Keeping the outside of your instrument clean is very simple. There are all kinds of treated cloths and even polishing gloves that not only clean your instrument, but make it shine too. Some even leave a thin film that protects it against sweat and dirt. Of course, a regular cotton cloth with a little instrument cleaner will do the job as well.

Lacquer or silver

There are different types of cloths, gloves, and cleaners for lacquered and silver-plated instruments, and only a few that you can use for both. Using the wrong type may damage your lacquer or plating.

Polish

Ordinary silver polish or brass polish is less expensive than most polishes sold in music shops, but it isn't the same stuff: It's usually way too abrasive and therefore may leave scratches or remove the lacquer finish.

> ### Blacker is better
>
> *Silver polishing cloths get very black in time. Contrary to what you might think, the blacker they get, the more effective they'll be. Washing a silver polishing cloth turns it into an ordinary piece of cloth, so don't. Silver-plated instruments should be polished very rarely in order to avoid wearing down the extremely thin plating.*

Valve covers

If you have very acidic perspiration, you may find dull spots where you hold the instrument. Slip-on *valve covers* or *valve guards* are designed to counteract this effect. They're available in a wide variety of designs, ranging from stars and stripes to skulls and bones, both in imitation leather (vinyl) and genuine leather. Similar covers are available for trombones. Do note, however, that your perspiration may be absorbed by the cover, where it will permanently affect your instrument — so it may be wiser to simply wipe your instrument each time after playing.

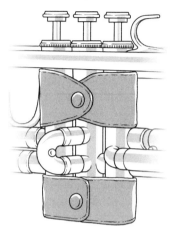

A valve cover, valve guard, or hand guard.

Duct tape

Many horn players have alternative ways to protect the vulnerable parts of their instruments, one of them being to wind them with duct tape. That won't look or feel as good as leather, however. You may also have trouble getting it off again after a while, so it's basically a stop-gap solution that only saves you no more than a couple of dollars.

VALVES AND SLIDES

Perfectionists may use six or seven different lubricants for the various parts of their instrument. After all, valve slides shouldn't move as easily as pistons; piston valves need a thinner type of oil than rotary valves, and so on. Still, other brass players happily make do with two different all-round lubricants. That is probably the minimum, though. There is no one 'best way' to lubricate your instrument. Just ask other horn players for their experiences and try a few different lubricants and methods yourself.

In advance

Some tips in advance:

- Most lubricants cost around **five dollars** per bottle, so that shouldn't stop you from experimenting a bit.

121

- Most people use too much oil, rather than too little. Usually, **one or two drops** will do. Excess oil and grease can be removed with a special degreaser.

- There are lubricants that use **no oil**. They're smooth and odorless, and can't stain your clothes. However, some say they're a bit slower than traditional lubricants: The valves don't come back as fast.

Valve oil

To keep your piston valves moving smoothly you need valve oil, a lubricant that is almost as runny as water. Some piston valve lubricants are as odorless as water too. How often you should oil your valves depends on many things: on the quality of the instrument, the piston and valve materials, and on the way your saliva affects the type of lubricant you use. This is yet another reason to experiment with various lubricants.

TIP

The perfect lubricant

If you piston valves get slow after an hour or so of playing, you may need another type of lubricant. Your saliva interacts with the lube you use, and the favorite lubricant of your teacher of your fellow band members may simply not work so well for you.

Right

You can lubricate your valves without taking the pistons out (see page 104), but it's better to remove them. Do so one by one, and be careful: They're hollow, and their thin walls are easily dented. First wipe the piston clean with a lint-free cloth, then apply three or four drops of oil to it and replace it with a light twisting motion. That way the oil will spread around the whole piston and the inside of the valve casing, and you can easily feel the piston guide or guides (see page 58–59) slot into place.

Wrong

If you don't reassemble the valve properly, or if you put pistons in the wrong casings, the instrument will either sound like a futile talking duck imitation, or like nothing at all. Two tips:

- Only tighten the valve cap after you've made sure that the piston has been **properly reassembled**. If you do remove all three pistons at once, remember which valve goes where. They are often numbered: If so, piston #1 is the one closest to the mouthpiece.

- Valve caps will stay in place if you tighten them **gently** by hand. Don't apply any force, and never use a wrench. If they get stuck nevertheless, go see your dealer.

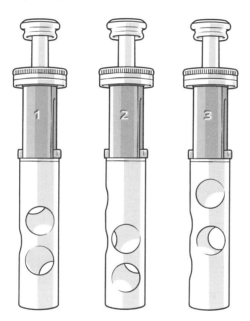

... see if they have numbers.

A little thicker

Some horn players find valve oil too runny, so they put a tiny bit of Vaseline on their valves. You're better off trying a slightly thicker type of oil, though, because Vaseline can eventually make your pistons stick.

Top cap felts

In the long run, the felt washers on top of the valves (*top cap felts*) will wear out. If they have become too thin, the pistons will go

123

down too far. As this happens very gradually, you may even not notice that the horn's resistance has increased over time.

Check

To check your felts, remove the second valve slide, depress the second valve, and look: The ports should be perfectly in line with the tubing. If the piston goes down too far, the felts need to be replaced.

Leadpipe

To protect your leadpipe and receiver from corrosion due to the acids in your saliva, occasionally trickle a few drops of valve oil into them. A tiny drop on the thread of each valve cap will prevent them from getting stuck.

One of the lubrication points on an F-at- tachment.

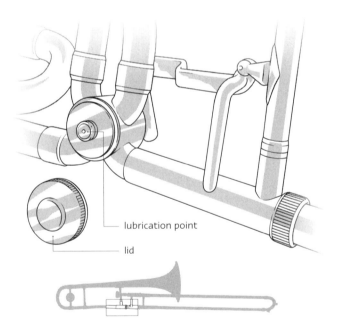

Rotary valves

Rotary valves need a slightly heavier lubricant. Rotors can be lubricated from the outside. Most of them require you to first unscrew a cap on one side and a screw on the other, but you don't need to dismantle it entirely.

124

Through the tube

You can also lubricate rotary valves by removing the appropriate slide and trickling a few drops of oil into the tubing that leads to the rotor. The oil will distribute best if you then operate the valve for a little while. A tip: Some companies offer a separate lubricant for the valve lever.

Tipcode TRP-018
This Tipcode provides a brief demonstration of lubricating a rotary valve.

String-action F-attachment

If you have a string-action F-attachment, check occasionally to make sure the string is not about to break, and be sure to always have a spare string with you, as well as the required tool or tools (usually a screwdriver will do) and a sketch of how to fit the string.

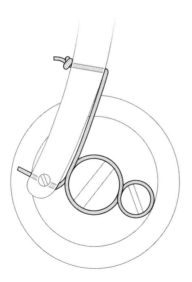

How to fit a string to an F-attachment.

125

Without a proper illustration, fitting a string is nearly impossible — even for some experienced players. Check if there's one in your instrument's manual. The illustration shown here may deviate from the one you need for your instrument.

Valve slides

Valve slides, on trumpets, cornets, and flugelhorns, should not slide as easily as the pistons. Therefore, slide oil or slide grease is less runny than valve oil. Because you use them while you play, the adjustable valve slides need to move a little more easily than the tuning slide or the second valve slide. Some brands have lighter and heavier types of slide oil for that purpose; others offer special tuning-slide oil.

Alternatively

You can also use the same slide oil for all the slides, and make the first and third valve slides a bit faster by using some valve oil as well. A tuning slide that moves of its own accord needs a heavier lubricant. Can the crook of a slide be removed? Then lubricate it occasionally, before it gets stuck.

Lubricate, twist, replace

Remove the valve slide you want to lubricate from your instrument, carefully clean it with a soft, dry cloth and lubricate both inner tubes. Wipe away the excess oil so that it doesn't end up inside the instrument. Slide one of the inner tubes into its outer tube and twist it a couple of times to distribute the lubricant over the entire surface. Now take it out again, and do the same with the other end. Then put the slide back on. Usually there's only one way it'll fit. If you do it the wrong way around, the slide won't go in all the way, or not at all.

Trombone slide cream

The trombone slide requires its own lubricant. Use trombone slide cream daily on new slides, lowering this frequency once the instrument is broken in.

Skin cream

Trombonists, like other brass players, often experiment with

alternative solutions. Some swear by certain types of furniture polish or skin cream instead of dedicated trombone slide cream. Again: When you consider how long it lasts, a jar of dedicated slide cream isn't that expensive — and you can be confident it will always work well.

Never

The slide itself is only around a hundredth of an inch (0.25 mm) thick, so it dents and bends easily. To lubricate it, dismantle it carefully and lay the outer slide in your case. Wipe the tubes clean one by one, always toward the ends. A tip: Never hold one tube while you are cleaning or lubricating the other, to prevent bending them.

Rotate the tube

Next, spread a little cream around the first tube and wipe off the excess. Stick the tube into the outer slide and rotate it a few times. Take it off, and do the same with the second tube. If you're going to play right away, spray on a little water and go (see page 104).

The fast way

Some trombonists prefer to lubricate only the first half of both tubes, and then move the slide in and out a few times. That way there's less chance of dented and bent tubes, and the cream will spread around the slide anyway as you play.

Other parts

Now and again dab a little cream on the bell lock, the mouthpiece shank, and the slide lock. That way you'll avoid anything getting terribly stuck.

INSIDE

If you really want to do a proper job, you need to clean the inside of your instrument every two or three months. Your mouthpiece,

127

receiver, and leadpipe require a little extra attention more often, as they are the first parts to get clogged up by whatever you blow into the instrument.

Mouthpiece

If you don't clean your mouthpiece now and then, its bore will gradually get smaller and smaller. Rinsing it under the tap (lukewarm or cold water only) after every rehearsal, concert, or practice session is a good start. It's good practice to clean the mouthpiece with a special mouthpiece brush and a mild soap solution about once a week. A liquid detergent will do just fine. Continue pulling the brush through the mouthpiece until it comes out clean.

Bowl

Remove scale by putting your mouthpiece in a bowl of water with a good dash of vinegar once every few weeks. Another cleaning trick is to soak your mouthpiece for a few hours in water with a bit of liquid detergent. Some horn players will even dissolve some baking soda in a pan and boil their mouthpiece in it. Warning: If you want to try this, always rinse your mouthpiece with lots of cold water before touching it: Brass gets very hot and doesn't cool off quickly.

Big tub

To clean the inside of your instrument, it's handy if you have a tub big enough to submerge it completely. Lay a towel on the bottom of the tub to prevent scratches, put your horn in (pistons should be removed), and fill the tub with lukewarm water. A trombone should always be bathed in three sections, preferably one at a time: the bell, the inner slide, and the outer slide. Rotary valves can stay in place.

Detergents

You may add a little mild shampoo or dish washing detergent to the water. Do not use anything that may be more aggressive than soapy water. Some even consider a liquid detergent too much, but others have been using it for years. If you add anything, make sure to thoroughly rinse the instrument afterwards.

Running water

If you don't have a big enough tub, allow some lukewarm water to run through each tube for little while. You can also do this to clean the receiver and leadpipe only. For that purpose, just take the tuning slide off (the hand slide, for trombone players).

> ### Too hot
> Warning: If the water is too hot, you may burn yourself as you touch the instrument. Also, hot water may damage a lacquer finish.

Trombone slide

To clean a trombone slide, you can fill it up with warm water and move it up and down a couple of times. If you added shampoo or soap to the water, you need to rinse it with clear water afterwards.

Cleaners, snakes, and brushes

The wet tubing of you instrument can be cleaned inside using a bore cleaner or *snake*: a flexible coiled spring or nylon string with a hard brush or a sponge at one or both ends. *Tip:* frequently check the condition of you flexible brush to prevent it from breaking inside the instrument. Replace the brush in due time.

A bore cleaner, a valve brush, and a mouthpiece brush.

Valve casings and portholes

Similar brushes are available to clean the valve casings and the pistons' portholes. Alternatively, you can pull a clean, lint-free cotton cloth through them a couple of times.

Spit balls

Another way to clean the inside of your instrument is to use

129

Spit Balls. These are small foam balls that you blow through the tubing.

Drying and lubricating
Rinse out all the tubes again when they are clean. Carefully shake and blow out as much water as you can, dry the outside, and leave everything until the inside is dry too. Then lubricate the valves and the slide(s), and don't forget to apply a tiny drop of oil to the shank of your mouthpiece, the inside of the leadpipe, and the moving parts of the water keys.

Scale and tarnish
To properly remove scale and tarnish from the inside of the instrument, you'll need to get it thoroughly cleaned by a professional (see page 131).

Maintenance sets
Many brands sell complete maintenance sets that contain various brushes, a cleaning cloth, lubricants, and sometimes even spare parts such as felts for the valves, or water key corks.

PROBLEMS

If your instrument is dented, if a brace has come loose, or if your mouthpiece, a valve, a slide, or anything else is stuck, the best advice is to take it to a technician. Bending, soldering, or using wrenches or other tools on your instrument is always risky, not least because brass instrument have very thin walls.

Stuck mouthpiece
You can sometimes get a stuck mouthpiece loose by running plenty of cold water over it. Wrapping a cloth around it will give you more grip. If that doesn't work, get it to a technician, who will use a special mouthpiece puller. Should your instrument not fit its case or bag with the mouthpiece attached, wrap it in a towel for the time being.

Jammed slide

If a valve slide is jammed, you may try to pull it out with a cloth, which you push through the bow. Be careful not to damage anything when the slide lets go: Keep hold of it when you pull. If you think you need to pull too hard, have a technician do it for you.

Tipcode TRP-019
Here's how you can remove a jammed slide with a cloth.

TIPCODE

Overhaul

A proper overhaul is a job for a professional too. This includes replacing felts, springs, and corks, smoothing out dents, polishing the instrument, and everything else it needs to perform properly for another one, two, or three years. The latter mostly depends on how often you play and what you do to keep your horn clean. A complete overhaul also includes a special bath to remove inside scale and tarnish, as well as relacquering or replating the instrument, which will make it as good as new. This will usually set you back some two hundred fifty to three hundred fifty dollars or more.

131

10

History

The trombone hasn't changed much over the last four centuries and even the valved trumpet is a good hundred and fifty years old. To meet their very earliest ancestors, you need to go back thousands of years.

Lip-vibrated wind instruments made of shells, hollowed-out pieces of wood, and other materials have been around for thousands of years. Horns have been made out of animal horns as well; the double meaning of the word 'horn' is no coincidence. The instrument below has toneholes that allow you to play different pitches.

A horn literally made of horn. Note the toneholes.

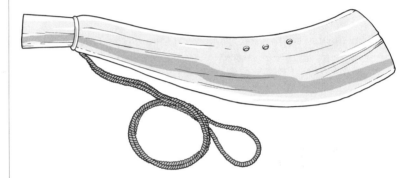

Bronze, gold, silver

Only much later did the first metal variations appear, made of bronze, gold, or silver, for instance. Early metal trumpets were usually no more than a long straight tube, slightly wider at one end (the 'bell'), with the other end (the 'mouthpiece') flattened slightly for the lips.

A few examples

Over the centuries, just about every culture has had its own trumpets. From the Greek *salpinx*, the bronze Celtic *carnyx*, and the Roman *lituus*, over two thousand years ago, to the medieval European *buisine* and the fifteen-foot long, copper Tibetan *dung* — and those are just a few examples.

Bends without kinks

Only some six hundred years ago did craftsmen learn how to bend tubes without getting kinks in them. By then, the trumpet gradually began to assume its modern form. It was still without valves, though, so it could play only a limited number of different notes (see page 6). These types of horns are known as *natural instruments*.

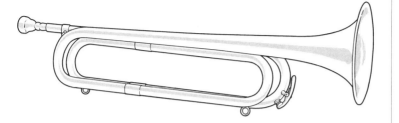

Slide trumpet

Not much later, someone came up with the *slide trumpet*, which allowed more notes to be played. It was awkward to play, as you had to slide the entire instrument backwards and forwards. The trombone (Italian for large trumpet), introduced a little later, was a much better solution. Some of the earliest trombones, made more than four centuries ago, are remarkably similar to the modern-day instrument.

The first valves

In the eighteenth century, an anonymous instrument maker devised a system of keys for the trumpet, but it wasn't ideal. The breakthrough for brasswind instruments was introduced in 1815, when the German craftsmen Blühmel and Stölzel presented the first valve, which looked something like a metal matchbox. In 1839, the Frenchman Périnet added a few improvements, and piston valves have been known as *Périnet valves* ever since. A few years earlier, the Austrian trumpet maker Riedl had invented the rotary valve.

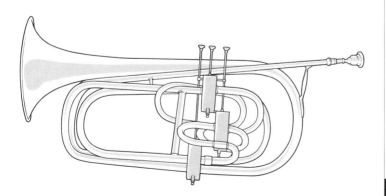

The earliest valves resembled matchboxes.

135

The flugelhorn

Originally, the flugelhorn was a small horn played by the horsemen who rode on the far left and right flanks (Flügel, in German) of a hunting party. Some early flugelhorns had keys, like a saxophone, and around 1850 the first flugelhorns with valves appeared. Who invented the modern flugelhorn will never be entirely clear: Numerous instrument makers came up with numerous designs and variations over the years, finally resulting in the present-day design. The original valveless flugelhorn, commonly referred to as bugle, is still being used.

The cornet

Cornet means 'little horn.' The short cornet, originally, is a small French or German horn with valves added. In the US, players preferred a somewhat brighter, crisper sound, and so the long American cornet was designed.

11

The Brass Family

*Essentially, all brass instruments are very much alike.
The main differences? The tubing may be longer or
shorter, it may be more or less conical, and there may
be one or more valves or a slide. That's about it. A brief
introduction to the most important family members.*

Many brass instruments come in various keys. One example, the C trumpet, was mentioned in Chapter 2. A little smaller are the soprano trumpets in D, E♭, or E. Another size smaller and higher is the sopranino. The very smallest and highest-sounding model is the *piccolo trumpet* or *Bach trumpet*, in A and B♭.

Piccolo trumpet.

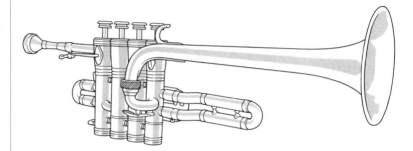

Larger trumpets

There are lower-sounding trumpets too. In F, for example, or the *bass trumpet* in B♭, which has the same range as a tenor trombone. Compared to the bore size of a standard trumpet (around 0.460"), a bass trumpet is a much wider instrument (e.g., 0.485"), with a much lager bell (some 7 instead of around 5").

Two tunings

Smaller trumpets often can be pitched in two keys, and some even in three. If you buy a G/F trumpet, for instance, it will probably come with two leadpipes, a set of extra valve slides, and an extra tuning slide, or even a second bell. When you are playing in F you use the longer tubes and valve slides, and if you need a G trumpet you use the shorter ones, which raises the pitch. Besides these trumpets, there are also flugelhorns that can be used in C and D,

TIP

Four valves

Piccolo trumpets often have four valves, and some flugel-horns do too. The fourth valve lowers the key by a fourth (from B♭ to F, for instance), just like an F-attachment on a trombone.

138

for instance. The more extra parts you get with it, the better the intonation of the instrument can be in both keys.

Pocket-sized

The *pocket trumpet* looks smaller than it is. If you were to roll it out, it would be just as long as a regular B♭ trumpet, and it sounds the same pitch too, believe it or not. Pocket-sized cornets are also available.

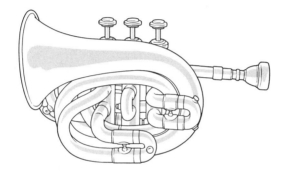

A pocket trumpet sounds bigger than it looks.

Rotary valves and rotary trumpets

Trumpets with rotary valves, commonly known as *rotary trumpets*, are still popular in some countries, mainly in Germany.

German trumpets

The valves are not the only difference. Rotary trumpets also have a very large bore, for example. Their big, powerful and warm sound makes them very suitable for the symphonic works of German composers. Rotary trumpets are most popular in that country, and accordingly they're also known as *German trumpets*. Conversely,

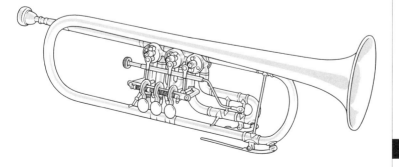

A rotary trumpet.

139

*An Aïda
trumpet with
three valves.*

*A cimbasso
is an Italian
contrabass
trombone.*

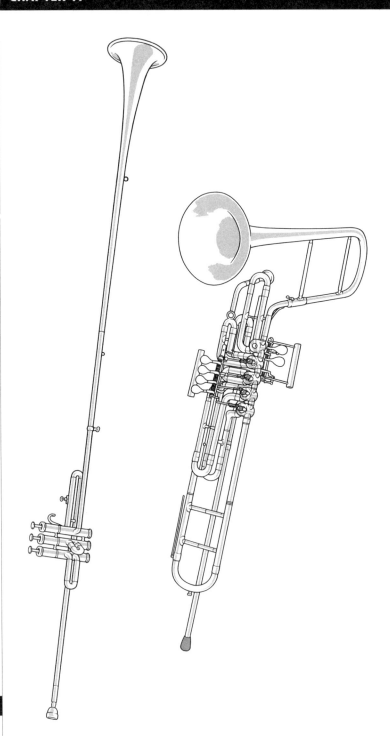

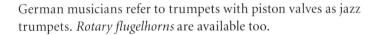

German musicians refer to trumpets with piston valves as jazz trumpets. *Rotary flugelhorns* are available too.

Variations

There are many, many more trumpet variations, such as 'stereo' instruments with two bells; or stretched instruments like Fanfare, Herald, or Triumphal trumpets, or the equally stretched Aïda trumpet from Verdi's 1871 opera.

And more

Many other lip-vibrated instruments, which all belong to the trumpet family, can be found in other cultures, ranging from side-blown horns (found in Africa, for instance) to the alphorn.

Smaller and larger trombones

Besides the tenor, alto, and bass trombones, there are various smaller and larger instruments. The *soprano trombone* or *mini trombone* has the same range as a trumpet, sounding an octave higher than a tenor trombone. The rare *piccolo trombone* sounds another octave higher, and the even rarer *piccolini* sounds two octaves higher. Thein is one of the few companies that makes these instruments. Two more uncommon horns are the *contrabass trombone* and the *cimbasso*, the Italian contrabass.

A bit of everything

A few more variations:

- The discontinued Holton **Superbone** had two piston valves, like a trumpet, but it also has a slide, like a trombone.

- The Kanstul **Flugelbone** looks like a flugelhorn but sounds like a trombone.

- The **flumpet** is a cross between a flugelhorn and a trumpet.

BACKGROUND BRASS

The instruments in this book belong to what's known as *soprano*

141

A bass tuba in
B-flat (B♭).

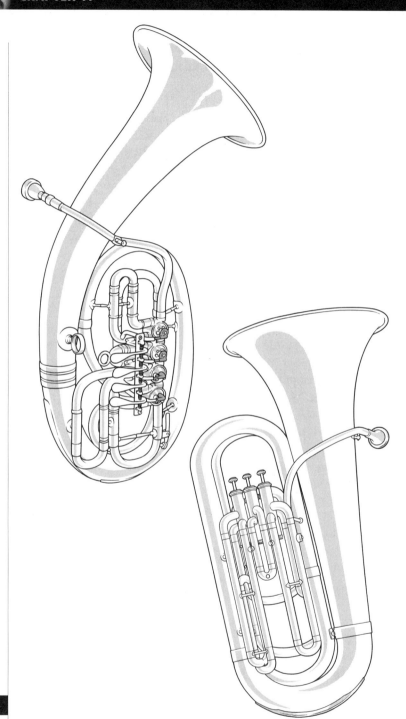

An oval-
shaped
baritone,
German
model
(Steyr).

142

or *treble brass* — the higher-pitched brass instruments — as opposed to the so-called low brass instruments. The bass trombone is a low brass instrument, and so are the *alto horn*, the *tuba* and the *euphonium*, among others. Most of these instruments are also known as *background brass*, i.e., instruments that are mainly used to accompany the melody instruments, and hardly ever for solos. They often have more valves, up to six, and they all have a markedly conical, widely-flared tube.

Tuba
The name tuba usually refers to the bass tuba, which has a tube around twenty-five feet long. Bass tubas come in C, for symphony orchestras, and in B♭, for brass, concert, and other wind bands. One size smaller are tubas pitched in F and E♭. These low pitches are often indicated as CC ('double C'), BB♭ ('double B-flat'), FF, and EE♭, respectively.

Euphonium
The t*enor tuba*, pitched one octave higher than the bass tuba, is usually referred to as euphonium.

Saxhorns
Around 1845, when Adolphe Sax was still perfecting his saxophone, he was granted a patent on a whole family of *saxhorns*, from large to small. A few of those instruments are still in use, such as the *tenor horn* and the *baritone*. The baritone is very similar to the euphonium, but a euphonium has a wider bore and a larger bell, and as a result sounds somewhat bigger and warmer. The two lowest-sounding saxhorns are pretty much the same instruments as the large B♭ and E♭ tubas.

TIP

Confusing
Many brass instruments have different names in different countries: A tenor horn is called alto or althorn by some, and baritone by others, for example. Another difference: German saxhorns look quite different because of their oval shape, but they sound the same, basically.

143

French horn

Brass instruments are often called horns, but the only 'real' horns have a circular main tube. The *French horn*, a very distinctive instrument, is most often found in symphony orchestras, concert bands, and brass bands. The *mellophone* is very similar to this instrument. The *hunting horn* has no valves (see page 107).

A French horn has a circular main tube and rotary valves.

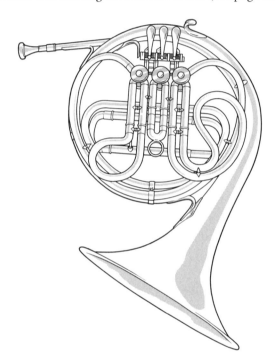

OTHER RELATIVES

The brass family is much bigger still. For instance, there are special designs for marching bands, such as the impressive *sousaphone*, and there is a whole group of natural instruments.

Marching instruments

Ordinary tubas, horns, and trombones are tricky to play if you're marching. That's why many special models have been designed. A well-known example is the sousaphone: a 'circular tuba' with

144

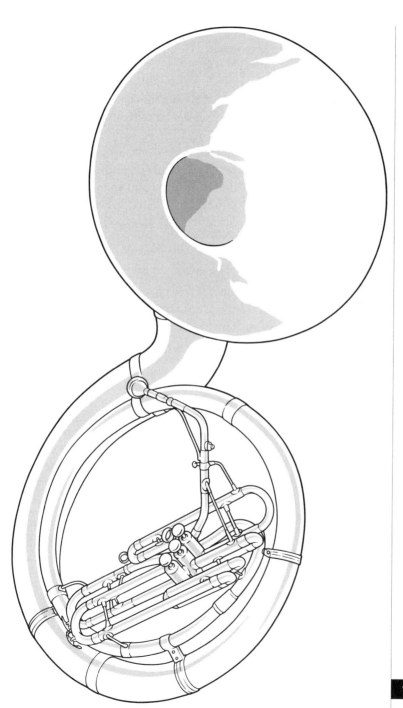

Very low: a sousaphone.

an enormous, forward-facing bell that is often made of a lighter, synthetic material to save weight.

On your shoulder

You can also get trumpet-shaped euphoniums, horns, and mellophones, and tubas that are designed so that you can rest them on your left shoulder, making them easier to march with. The bells of these instruments point forwards instead of upwards, so the sound is projected toward the audience. Some companies make *convertible instruments*: You switch from an upright tuba to a marching instrument by removing the valve section, turning the instrument around, and reinstalling the valves section.

Without valves

Instruments without valves can play harmonics only. They're referred to as natural instruments (see pages 6 and 134). Some examples are the natural trumpet or clarion, the hunting horn, and the bugle. You see such instruments in army bands, for instance, and of course in drum & bugle corps. (Regulation) bugles may have one or more slides or valves.

Bach

Valveless instruments are also used in concert halls. When Bach (1685–1750) wrote the Second Brandenburg Concerto, valves hadn't been invented yet. Some musicians still prefer to play this work on the traditional valveless *baroque trumpet* or *Bach trumpet*.

TIP

And what about the sax?

You'd think a saxophone was a brasswind instrument, with its brass body that gets progressively wider. However, instead of valves, saxophones have a key mechanism, like clarinets and flutes. The mouthpiece is also taken from the clarinet. So, although it is a wind instrument made of brass, the sax belongs to the woodwind family — like the flute, in fact, even though most flutes are metal instruments.

146

12

How They're Made

Some companies still make their instruments almost entirely by hand, while others leave most of the work to computer-controlled machines. Here's a quick look at some of the processes used in the production of brass instruments.

Most higher-priced instruments have one-piece bells, made of a single sheet of brass. The sheet is cut precisely to size and folded double, after which the seam is soldered.

A two-piece bell before assembly.

A flat sheet of brass (1), folded (2), rolled (3), roughly hammered into shape (4 and 5), bent, and finished (6) (Kanstul).

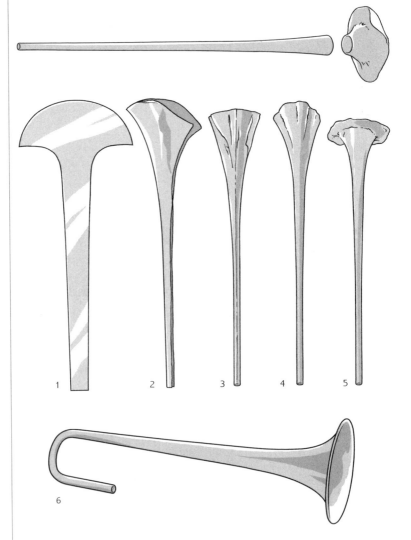

Hammers

Traditionally, wooden hammers are used to hammer the bell in shape against a steel mandrel. To make hammering the brass easier, it is first rolled in a mill. The resulting shape roughly resembles a run-over flower, as shown in illustration as shown in the illustration (#3). In some factories, the hand-hammering has been taken over by machines.

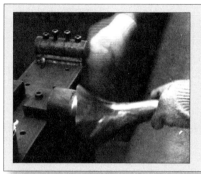

Tipcode TRP-020

This final Tipcode takes you on a brief tour to a brasswind factory, where you will see — among other things — how a bell is hammered into shape.

TIPCODE

Two parts

The widest part (the flare) of a two-piece bell is made by pressing a small, fast-spinning brass disc in shape against a mandrel, using a tool that very closely resembles a baseball bat. New welding techniques (plasma welding) can make two-piece bells behave like they were seamless, one-piece bells.

The bends

To prevent the tubes from kinking when they are bent, they are first filled. In the past, molten lead would be used. Today it's more likely to be sand, or a soap solution that is frozen inside the tube.

Bullets

Shorter bend tubes, like the second valve slide, are made perfectly round on the inside by forcing steel balls through them.

By hand

Traditionally, valves and pistons are assembled by hand, one at a time. A single piston is made out of four tubes: the piston itself and the three ports that run through it.

Fit

Before the instrument is finished, all the sliding parts must be made to fit precisely. The more expensive the instrument, the

149

lower the tolerances: a tighter fit, while still running smoothly. Pistons and slides are often hand-lapped for this purpose.

Assembly

Finally the instrument is buffed to a shine and lacquered or plated, assembled, checked, and shipped. Lacquered instruments are usually baked to increase the hardness of the finish.

Lathe

Mouthpieces are made largely on a lathe. The mouthpiece itself turns and a sharp blade takes away the metal that has to be removed. Sometimes the chisel is guided by hand, but usually a computer does this job.

13

Brands

There are dozens of companies making brass instruments — from one-man workshops to large factories. This chapter introduces you to the main brand names, as well as to some of the lesser-known ones.

Most of the larger, well-known companies produce all four of the instruments covered in this book, as well as other brasswinds. They typically concentrate on intermediate and professional horns. Some of them also make instruments or parts for other brands. This chapter starts with a brief description of some of those companies, followed by an introduction to a number of generally smaller makers, which often focus on a specific price range — either student, intermediate or professional.

Time sensitive

Please do note that the information in this chapter is relatively time sensitive. Companies can be sold, formerly high-end brand names may at one time be used on low-budget instruments, new brands can be introduced, and product lines can be expanded, limited, or discontinued. Still, most of the names below have been and will be around for years to come.

Where it's made

Many companies have instruments made in different places. For example, it's not uncommon for US companies to have all (or the lower-budget part) of their horns made in China, according to their specifications. Likewise, there are Asian (and American and European) brasswind makers that produce instruments for various brands, and you may come across identical horns with different brand names and price tags. Of course, the same happens with guitars, pianos, and all other instruments.

The Austrian trumpet player and engineer Vincent Bach made his first mouthpieces in 1918 after moving to New York. About six years later he built his first trumpet. Today, the Bach name can be found on a wide variety of brass instruments and accessories.

152

The brands named after trumpet player Elden Benge, cornetist Charles Conn, and trombonist Thomas King all belong to the American Conn-Selmer company. Still, they're bascially three separate brands, each offering instruments in various price ranges. Holton and Leblanc are Conn-Selmer brands too. Both companies used to make various brasswind instruments but now focus on French horns and clarinets respectively.

GETZEN®

T.J. Getzen opened a repair workshop in New York in 1939. A couple of years later he started making his own horns. The company is still family-owned. DEG (Dynasty) and Edwards (see below) were founded by Getzen descendants.

JUPITER®

Jupiter is one of the world's larger woodwind and brasswind instrument brands. All instruments are made by KHS, the Taiwanese parent company that was founded in 1930. The same company also makes Mapex drums.

Zigmant Kanstul learned his trade under at the now defunct F. E. Olds Company. Prior to founding Kanstul Musical Instruments in

153

1981, he also worked for King, being in charge of the Benge plant, and for Conn. Kanstul builds instruments for other companies as well.

The one-man organ factory founded by Torakusu Yamaha in 1889 is now the world's biggest manufacturer of musical instruments, from brasswinds and woodwinds to guitars, pianos, home keyboards, and drums. The Japanese company also makes motorbikes, hi-fi equipment, and other products.

More US brands

There are many American brasswind companies. The following typically focus on professional instruments only, their prices starting around two, three, or even five thousand dollars, in some cases going up to more then ten. Well-known names are **Blackburn**, **Calicchio** (hand-made in California), **Edwards** (by Edward Getzen, of the Getzen family), **Harrelson**, **Marcinkiewicz** (makes mouthpieces too), **Miles**, **Monette**, **Shires**, and **Schilke** (trumpets and trombones; makes mouthpieces too). A few companies specialize on trombones. Examples include **Greenhoe** (US), **Rath** (UK), and the German companies **Frost** and **Schmelzer**.

Student and intermediate

Various US and international companies mainly market student and lower-priced intermediate instruments, which are almost always Asian made. Brand names include **Barrington**, **Blessing**, **Burbank**, Bundy (a brand name of the former Bach company, now owned by Conn-Selmer), **Etude**, **F.E. Olds**, **Kohlert**, and **Prelude**. Others make a range from low-budget to professional instruments, such as the Brazilian Weril company.

Intermediate and up

The most affordable instruments from companies such as **Eastman**, **Giardinelli**, **Fides**, **W. Nirschl** are at a somewhat higher price level, while US companies **Holton**, **Leblanc** (originally

154

from France), and **Sonare** (a German-US product) focus on intermediate to professional horns.

Germany

Most European brass instrument manufacturers can be found in Germany, where many companies specialize in background brasswinds, but they make trumpets and other horns as well. All or most of these instruments are in the professional price range. **B&S** (Challenger), **Cannonball** (a US company), **VMI**, and **Scherzer** are four brands that come from the same factory, B&S, in Markneukirchen. **Alexander**, best known for its French horns, makes a flugelhorn/trumpet combination as well. Some other German brass wind makers are **Glassl**, **Kühnl & Hoyer**, **Miraphone**, and **Thein**, the latter producing a wide range of trombones, from the small piccolino to the contrabass. The production of **Galileo** trumpets moved from Germany to the Egger company in Switzerland.

Other European companies

Most other European companies also focus on higher-level intermediate and professional instruments. Here are some examples.

- Antoine **Courtois** (known for the Evolution trumpet, but active in all price ranges), **Couesnon**, and **Henri Selmer Paris** (best-known for their saxophones, but makes professional trumpets and cornets too) are from France. Besson originally came from France, but later moved to England. The French Besson series are made in the US.

- **Stomvi**, from Spain, also produces mouthpiece kits with interchangeable cups.

- The Swiss **Willson** company makes flugelhorns, and trombones with their own Rotax valves.

- Two Austrian companies are **Schagerl** and **Haagston**, the latter offering custom made hammered and non-hammered instruments, with a choice of leadpipes, finishes, and metals.

- **Taylor** and **Wedgwood** brasswinds are hand-made in England.

155

- The Czech **Amati** company produces budget and mid-range woodwinds and brasswinds. **Cerveny**, mainly focusing on background brass, is a brand name of the same company.

- **Van Laar**, from the Netherlands, makes professional trumpets and flugelhorns.

- **Adams**, another Dutch company, also makes euphoniums.

14

Orchestras and Bands

As a horn player, there are all kinds of bands, orchestras, ensembles, and other lineups you can choose to play in. Here's a short introduction to some of the main groups you can join.

Of course, brasswinds are essential in all the various types of high school and college bands: marching bands that perform either onstage, in parades, or during football games; pep bands, which often also feature a set drummer and an electric bass guitar; wind bands, with brasswinds and woodwinds, including oboes and bassoons; or concert bands, with some sixty to more than a hundred band members. A concert band lineup includes all the brasswinds (soprano and background brass), woodwinds (flute, saxophones, clarinets, oboes, and so on), and a traditional percussion setup.

Brass bands and more

As a brass player, you can also join a brass band, of course (the cornet plays an important role here), or a drum & bugle corps, or a community band. If you want brass only, there are brass choirs, and you may also want to join a trombone choir or a trumpet choir. Choirs often play classical or contemporary music, either specifically composed for or adapted to the lineup. Other brasswind ensembles may consist of two trumpets, two French horns, and two or three trombones; or four trumpets, three trombones, and a bass trombone. Brasswind quintets have various lineups: Two trumpets, one trombone, a French horn, and tuba is just one example.

Symphony orchestra

The biggest classical orchestra, the symphony orchestra, may contain over a hundred musicians. The violinists are the largest group. Larger orchestras often have five trumpet players and three or four trombonists, along with other brass players (French horn, tuba, and so on), woodwind players (flute, clarinet, etc.), percussionists, harpists, and a pianist. Chamber orchestras are much smaller.

Other formats

Classical music — and many other styles of music as well — can be played in numerous other lineups, which perform compositions that were written specifically for or adapted to the instruments used. Some examples include works for one, two, or three brasswinds with piano, or with strings and harpsichord, or with

tympani only, or with an equal number of violins, or works for solo trumpet and solo voice, or an ensemble that consists of trumpet, two violins, flute, and French horn.

Jazz

The cornet was especially popular in the first jazz bands, which sprang up in the early 1900s. You still find them in Dixieland bands. Later, the trumpet gained the upper hand. A mainstream or bebop jazz quintet usually consists of a trumpet player, a saxophonist, a pianist, a bassist, and a drummer. Most big bands have four trumpeters, four trombonists, several saxophonists, and of course a pianist, a bassist, and a drummer. High school and college jazz bands may have even more instrumentalists.

Funk and rock

Horn players may feature in all kinds of other popular bands, supplying fancy lines, colorful accents, and sizzling riffs. A typical wind section, with two saxophonists, a trumpeter, and a trombonist, may play any style from jazz dance to salsa, from soul to African pop.

International folk music

You can also join one of the many ensembles that play the folk music of different countries and cultures, ranging from Mexican mariachi bands to German-oriented polka bands and Jewish klezmer groups, and so on!

15

Tips on Practicing

Practicing doesn't seem to be every musician's favorite pastime, and that goes for musicians at all levels and ages. Why? Because most musicians want to play their favorite music, rather than spending hours playing scales, etudes, or arpeggios. Because, oftentimes, progress doesn't show right away. And because learning to play an instrument is about long-term gratification, and we seem to have lost touch with that concept. Or because of any number of reasons. But still, it needs to be done — and it can be entertaining, too!

This chapter offers helpful hints on how to practice efficiently, turning practice sessions into rewarding and even inspiring events. Ineffective practice habits are as much work as effective ones, but yield no progress and may cause you to quit playing entirely. Also included in this chapter are helpful tips on where and when to practice, the various components of a good practice session and how to structure it, practice techniques, the importance of memorizing music, and much more.

Sports

Practicing is to music what training is to sports, but there are some major differences. Firstly, most sportsmen train with their teammates, while practicing is something you usually do alone. Secondly, if you play football, soccer, or any other type of sport, you'll probably have a match every week. Most musicians don't have that many opportunities to perform — and usually, being able to perform is why you practice in the first place.

Joining a band

That's why it's important to play in a band, an ensemble, or an orchestra: This offers performance opportunities, it's a great way to meet new friends, and it provides you with clear and realistic goals. Practicing so you can play your part at the next rehearsal is a better motivation than practicing because, well, you're supposed to.

One note

Joining an ensemble is even more important if your play violin, trumpet, flute, clarinet, or any of the other instruments that typically produce one note at a time. These instruments are best suited for group settings, or should at least be accompanied by a piano, for example.

Chords

The piano, keyboards, and guitars are better suited to playing just by yourself, without a band or another form of accompaniment — but even then, playing with other musicians is both fun and inspiring.

Keep on going

162

It's clear that practice is necessary to achieve a certain level. But

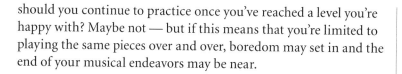

should you continue to practice once you've reached a level you're happy with? Maybe not — but if this means that you're limited to playing the same pieces over and over, boredom may set in and the end of your musical endeavors may be near.

No practicing

So can you play without practicing? Of course you can. There are thousands of garage band musicians who never practice; they just play with their friends, and they're having a ball doing so. However, they will usually stop playing once they get a little older, and having no real musical basis, it's unlikely that they'll pick up an instrument again later on in life.

Recreational music making

Participating in a drum circle, for example, allows anyone to play music with a group of people without any prior experience. These and other recreational music-making activities are about socializing, reducing stress, and relaxation more than striving for musical prowess. (Incidentally, that's what most garage bands are about, too.)

Not another obligation

If you want to pursue a career in music, your practice habits should foster diligence, hard work, and making sacrifices (though the latter may not be considered as such). If you don't, practicing should probably be more about fun than about obligations.

Means, goal, or making music?

Some tend to see practice as a goal in and of itself; and the goal is achieved by practicing, say, a half an hour a day. Others consider practice a means to an end — the end usually being the ability to play well (at whatever level) and to perform successfully. You can also consider practice as making music, as a journey that leads to who knows where, and the journey itself is what it's all about. Teachers who make you understand and feel that playing scales is essential will help you enjoy this journey.

163

How long — or how?

One of the most frequently asked questions is, 'How long should I practice?' You could certainly structure your practice sessions to last a required number of minutes per day. But wouldn't it be more interesting to look at what should or could be achieved, so your focus would be on accomplishing a particular task, rather than on filling time? Still, no matter how you look at it, you do need to invest some time in practice, and it's essential to be able to gauge how much time that typically is, so that's what the next section addresses.

The youngest musicians

For very young musicians, things are a bit different. Most experts seem to agree that you can't really speak of 'practicing' until kids are some five or six years of age. For these kids, it's more about spending quality time and having fun with their instrument (if they've actually already chosen one) than about trying to achieve something other than a long-lasting love for music. Playing up to five or ten minutes a day will be fine. The shorter these sessions last and the more fun they are, the more likely a child will want to play three, four, or more days per week.

Six and up

As children get a little older, they'll be able to focus for longer periods, and they'll start to grasp the concept of doing things now that will pay off later. They will also be ready to maintain a practice routine with their teacher's and your guidance. Six- to eight-year-olds should typically spend some fifteen minutes per day on an instrument, say four to six days per week. The older they get, the longer they will be able, and willing, to play.

Half an hour

If you're older — twelve and up — most teachers will probably tell you that playing half an hour a day will help you make sufficient progress to keep things interesting. If you practice effectively, however, you may be able to do your assignments in less time. (This can be so rewarding that you end up playing longer than you intended!)

Short and often

For kids, a practice session lasting a half an hour can be quite long,

164

though, and it may be better to divide the routine up into three ten-minute sessions, or even six sessions of five minutes each. You can do so yourself, too: Short sessions tend to be more effective, with improved retention and more focus.

Much longer

The better you get, the more you need to practice to progress and maintain your abilities at a desired level. Music majors often practice three to five hours a day. The longer you practice, the sooner you will find that not practicing decreases your musical abilities — so you have to keep up all, or most, of the time!

Music, not minutes

Rather than focusing on a certain amount of time you need to practice, you can look at what should or could be achieved by practicing so you can focus on a set goal (and the music) rather than at the minutes passing by. In order to do so, you must understand exactly what your teacher expects (or you need to be able to set your own goals), and you need to be able to self-assess whether you've achieved those goals.

Assignments

For teachers, this means that they need to be very explicit about their assignments. For example, rather than simply telling you to "learn to play that piece," they must state specific criteria, (*i.e.*, "play it with the metronome at 148 beats per minute," or "play a scale five times, without any mistakes, at a certain minimum tempo"). This way, you can simply tell when you've completed the assignment. If the teacher also conveys the practice techniques you need to most effectively reach the goals set for that week, practicing will be much more than a thirty-minute routine to be endured. It also puts things into your own hands, rather than in the clock's hands.

Your own teacher

Practicing is something that needs to be learned (and often

165

taught). When you practice alone, you're expected to catch your own mistakes, to discover what prompted them, to fix them, and to find a way to prevent them in the future. In effect, when you practice, you are your own teacher. That's not an easy thing to be, of course.

At home

And after all that, when you get to your next lesson or performance, you may find that you're not able to play what you could play at home. Or could you? Did you really hear everything that went wrong? Did you repeat everything to a point where you could even play it under pressure? Probably not — and playing in front of a teacher, your family, or any other type of audience is quite different from playing when there's no one around. This can be practiced too, though. Simply ask your roommate, your kids, friends, or anyone else to come listen to the new piece you have — hopefully — mastered. Getting experienced in playing for others is an important part of the learning process.

When

Ideally, practicing becomes a daily routine, something which is as natural as having dinner, or brushing your teeth. And just like most people have dinner or brush their teeth around the same time every day, practicing is more likely to become a natural part of the day when you do it at or around a set time. Spending time with your instrument on a regular basis may be more important than how much practice you actually do, initially.

Every day?

Should you practice every day? It's unlikely that anything you *have* to do seven days a week will be a lot of fun. That's why many experts will advise you that practicing five to six days will do to make sufficient progress.

Which day?

Sunday often sounds like a good day to skip practicing — but at the same time, it happens to be the day of the week that allows for more time to practice, and practicing on Sunday still leaves plenty of time for other activities.

A closer look

If you're having lessons, the day before your lesson is usually the worst one to skip. Also note that it's often very effective to have a short practice session right after your lesson or later that same day. This reinforces the lesson content, and it's a perfect opportunity to take a close look at your weekly assignments.

No time

If it's simply to busy for your intended practice routine, try to sit down and just play one of your favorite pieces, or something else you like to play, rather than not playing at all. Keeping in touch with your instrument is really important.

When?

For many people, it seems best to practice at a set time (such as before school, right after work, before or after dinner). Others prefer to schedule their practice time around other obligations. That way, they can play when they feel like it, rather than having to do so because it happens to be 6:00 PM. Here are some additional tips on planning practice sessions:

• **For students**: Practicing before doing homework provides a nice break between your academic activities, but it may be hard to focus on music if you have lots of homework to do.

• Waiting until **after homework** to practice may feel as if you're never finished; it's like one obligation after the other.

• Planning a practice session **before your favorite TV show** (which is then the reward for practicing) may be more successful than trying to get up and practice when the show is over.

Holidays

It's really important that you keep to your practice sessions during school holidays as well. If you don't touch your instrument for a couple of weeks, the first lessons and practice sessions after the holiday may be quite frustrating as you probably won't be able to play those same pieces anymore. You may consider a holiday practice schedule, though.

167

How?

People all have their own ways of handling assignments, most likely approaching them the same way they do other things in life. Teachers can help you apply your personal way of handling things to your practice sessions, making them as efficient as possible. Some examples

- If you're not good at **focusing your attention**, don't start three new pieces at once.

- If you're **afraid to start new pieces**, you may tend to keep on 'practicing' songs you already play very well — so you're dedicating time to practicing, but you're not likely to make any progress.

- If you're **not aware of the mistakes** you make, you will end up rehearsing those mistakes, and it'll be hard to reverse and 'deprogram' those errors. The solution is to learn how to evaluate your own playing before moving on.

WHERE

Ideally, you should be able to practice whenever you feel like it, without being hindered and without hindering others. A practice space needn't be large, just enough to accommodate you and your instrument. If there's room for the instrument to remain unpacked between practice sessions, no valuable time (or inspiration!) gets lost by having to unpack and assemble it before each practice. Ideally, again, you should be able to grab your instrument, tune it if necessary, and play. There are various types of floor-standing and wall-mounted stands on which string instruments, wind instruments, and other small instruments can sit unpacked and out of the way of people, pets, and other potential causes of damage. Special covers are also available to help protect your valuable investments against dust and airborne dirt.

Music stand

If you read sheet music, you will need a music stand. This

affordable piece of hardware promotes good posture (and prevents sore necks), provided it has been set up at the correct height. Nearly all music stands can be folded into a compact size, but it's easier if they can be left standing for the next practice session. This also enhances their life expectancy, as they may be quite flimsy. Do you need to bring a stand to lessons or recitals? Then invest in a second stand that you can take along, leaving the other one at home. Larger type gig bags and instrument cases often have an outer pocket for a music stand.

More on music stands

A basic music stand will set you back less than twenty dollars. *Tip:* Most music stands have two pivoting 'arms' that keep the sheet music in place and prevent music books from flopping closed. If yours doesn't, you can use a rubber band or clothes pins, or you can have your music books spiral-bound so that they stay open.

Two more tips:

• Next to black and chrome models, music stands are also available in **bright colors**.

• If you use your music stand at home a lot, consider buying a heavy duty **orchestra model**.

Light

Lighting in the room should be sufficient to see the music easily and clearly. An additional small lamp is usually all that takes. *Tip:* There are special lamps available for music stands specifically.

Stool or chair

A regular stool or chair will usually do. Pianists, keyboard players, drummers, and other musicians are better off using a special (preferably height-adjustable) stool or bench. Without it, posture may be bad and practicing can be tiresome.

Metronome

A metronome can help you develop your inner clock. It's also a great device to use when practicing entire pieces or difficult bits very slowly, and it can help you improve your speed on the

169

instrument step by step. Like any other tool, metronomes should be used wisely. Using one isn't a very good idea with a new piece, or when you're focusing on your tone, for example. Also, if you use it too often, you may become dependent on it. Metronomes are available starting at less than twenty dollars. Many electronic versions also sound a 440 Hz tuning tone (the standard A to which most instruments are tuned; see page 105).

Two mechanical metronomes and two electronic ones.

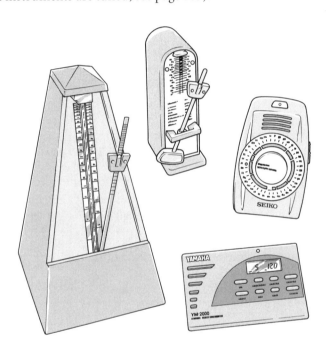

Sound systems and computers

Putting up a sound system in your practice area allows you to play along to prerecorded music, play back a recorded lesson, or record your practice sessions. Likewise, a computer can be used to play back CDs, DVDs, and CD-ROMS; to access Internet lessons and music games; or to record practice sessions (if equipped with the right hardware and software). It's also a helpful tool to compose, arrange, transpose, or create music. Synthesizers, home keyboards, and other digital instruments can be hooked up directly to the computer using MIDI, the musical instrument digital interface that is part of all digital music equipment.

170

And more

There's much more you can do to make practice more effective and fun. Here are some additional tips:

- Consider **lightening up** on practice arrangements if you're very busy. Play your instrument to relax rather than to study.

- Try playing in **another room** of the house from time to time, or even outside, if possible.

- Make sure your practice time is **uninterrupted**, and ask people who call to call back.

- **Varying the structure** of your practice sessions can help keep things fresh. Make your main focus playing a new piece for a month or so, then address sound production or intonation for a couple of weeks, and so on.

- If you want to practice an hour or more per day, do take one or more **short breaks**. Very brief micro-breaks help you stay focused. If you just can't get that one difficult passage down, comb your hair, pet the cat, eat a carrot, or take a sip of water before trying again. Or try again next week!

- Your instrument should be in **good repair** and tuned properly.

- **Stop if it hurts**. Playing an instrument should not induce pain. If the pain (back, fingers, neck, lips — anywhere) returns every time you practice or play, consult a teacher. The solution could be as simple as getting a different chair or resetting the music stand.

THE COMPONENTS

One of the main keys to effective practice is to have well-structured practice sessions. Depending on your level of playing, the main components of a practice session are:

- Warming up

- Scales and arpeggios

171

- Etudes

- Sight-reading

- New pieces

- Review

If you're a beginning student, the list will be shorter, and elements will be added as you progress.

Tuning
Most instruments need to be tuned, or the tuning needs to be checked, before you can play. This is where the practice session really begins. As said before, it is easiest if the instrument is always ready to be played — unpacked and assembled. You may want to have valuable and vulnerable instruments covered or packed when they're not being played, however. Also, parts such as strings, and the leather pads on woodwind instruments, tend to last longer if the instrument is covered between practice sessions.

Warming up
Playing music requires a warm up, just like sports do: You may even get injured if you play demanding pieces without a decent warm up. For beginners and intermediate players, the few minutes of 'warming up' are basically meant to get into mood for playing, to get the fingers going, and to get 'into the instrument.' In that sense, it even helps if you take a good long look at your instrument before you play your first notes. Warm-up exercises are not technically demanding; they're the ideal setting for focusing on tone quality, because you can really listen to the sound you're producing.

TIP

> ### Scales, arpeggios and etudes
> Scales and arpeggios are often used for warm ups, but they're also practiced separately. They're technical exercises that increase your playing proficiency, so your fingers will be able to do what your mind tells them to. Etudes are pieces written with that same goal in mind.

More fun

Many musicians dislike playing scales, etudes, and similar exercise material; it's not as much fun as 'real' pieces, and such exercises often seem meaningless. A good teacher may be able to make you understand why they're so essential, inspiring you to play them with all your heart (though a little less will usually do). Besides, there are various ways to make playing scales and etudes more fun. Some ideas?

- **Focusing on your tone** really helps; imagine what a scale would sound like when played by your all-time favorite musician!

- Playing scales as if they were **beautiful pieces of music** makes a difference too.

- Make the **volume go up** as you play the scale upwards, and vice versa.

- **Speed up** when playing upwards, and vice versa.

- Speed up and **get louder** one way, and vice versa.

- Play scales in the rhythm of **a song you like**, or play them as triplets.

New pieces

Adding new pieces is necessary to keep progressing, to keep yourself challenged, to expand your repertoire, and to raise your general level of playing. Check pages 177–179 for tips on handling new pieces.

Reviewing repertoire

When you play pieces you already know, there's no struggle, so you're simply playing music. It's as close to performing as practicing will get — and that's what playing is all about, for most musicians. Reviewing older pieces also keeps your repertoire alive.

Sight-reading

Sight-reading is as essential part of various exams and competitions: You're given a new and unfamiliar piece of music to read and play or sing on demand. It's much the same as reading a story or an article to someone, albeit that playing while reading music is quite a bit harder than reading text aloud. Sight-reading is an important skill for all musicians who want or need to play in situations where they will be expected to perform or rehearse without prior preparation.

And more

A practicing session can consist of lots of other components, such as:

- **Specific exercises** (dynamics, phrasing, improvisation, ear training, extending your range with higher notes, etcetera).

- **Experimenting**: Explore the instrument, try to discover new sounds or playing techniques, try to figure out a melody you've heard, think up new melodies.

- **Playing along** with prerecorded music or special play-along recordings. This is a valid, fun, and effective technique for any musician who doesn't have a band or an orchestra at their disposal. You can also record a performance or rehearsal of the band or orchestra you're in, and use that.

Recitals

Have you added a new piece to your repertoire and can you really play it? Again, try playing for friends or housemates. These brief, informal recitals can be very effective. They offer you an opportunity to perform, they may help diminish performance anxiety and they teach you to continue playing through mistakes — and you're most likely to make at least a few of those the first time you play a new piece.

TIP

Maintenance

Some instruments require a bit of maintenance at the end of each practice session. Wind instruments have to be disassembled and dried, orchestral string instruments will need the hair of their bows slackened, guitar and bass guitar strings need to be cleaned, and so on. Specific instructions can be found in the relevant chapter of this Tipbook.

174

STRUCTURE

To get the most out of your practice sessions, you need to structure them, planning ahead what it is you want to get done.

The beginning and the end
It's usually best to start with things that are relatively easy to play, such as scales. You may also prefer to start each session with a piece you already know. Starting off with an unfamiliar piece can be quite frustrating. Ending the session with a review of familiar repertoire is like a reward for having practiced.

The same order?
You may prefer the safety of doing things in the same order every time; others dislike such routine and rather vary the order of their practice components from day to day.

Two or three sessions
If you divide your practice time into two or more sessions, it's probably most effective to do a little of everything in each session rather then spending the first session only on scales, the second on a new piece, the third on older repertoire, etcetera — but then you might just prefer that.

Clock?
Some experts advise you to dedicate a certain amount of time to each component: a five minute warm-up, ten minutes or etudes, ten on a new piece, and another five to play something familiar. Others will tell you to get rid of the clock, as you want to focus on what you're playing rather than on the minutes passing by.

Short, medium, long
The clearer your musical goals are, the easier it will be to practice effectively. When defining these goals, it often helps to distinguish:

* **long-term goals**: I'd like to join such-and-such band, or play a solo recital by the end of the year or this month.
* **mid-term goals**: I'd like to finish this method book, or be able to play these pieces.

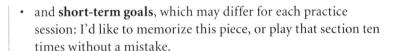
- and **short-term goals**, which may differ for each practice session: I'd like to memorize this piece, or play that section ten times without a mistake.

PRACTICING TECHNIQUES

Practicing efficiently is also a matter of applying the right practicing techniques. Improving your tone requires a different technique than increasing your speed, or tackling a new piece.

Small jobs
One of the best ways to make your practice session more effective and fun is to break down large jobs into a number of small jobs that you think you can easily manage. Rather than tackling a new piece from beginning to end, break it down into four or eight measures to be played per day, for example. This way, you can have a small success every day, rather than fighting to master the entire piece in one week. It works, really.

Revision
If a new piece is broken up into sections comprised of a number of bars, reviewing the sections that were done on previous days should be an essential part of each practice session. Learning an instrument is most effectively done through frequent repetition. (In various languages, the word for 'practice' literally means repetition!)

The right notes
Repetition results in long-term memory storage, which is good. The problem, however, is that your memory does not select what should be stored and what should not. If you consistently repeat an incorrect passage, that's what will be stored, and if you play the wrong note half of the time, there's a fifty-fifty chance that the wrong note will come out at your performance. So when repeating things, make sure you play the right notes — and slow down as much as you need on order to do so.

Five or ten

Some teachers may advise you to move to the next section only when you're able to play the current section correctly five (or ten) times in a row. If you make a mistake, you start counting all over again — until you get all five (or ten) correct. Others may not be concerned with the number of repetitions, so long as you play it right the final time: This way, your fingers are supposed to 'remember' the right moves.

Slow down

A difficult passage may be hard to play correctly, and playing it right five times in a row may seem impossible. The solution, again, is to slow things down. Slow, in this case, means really slow. Take one, two, or more seconds for every note, and disregard note values for now. Take a metronome, set it at sixty BPM (i.e., sixty Beats Per Minute, equaling one beat per second), and let it tick one, two, or more times before moving on to the next note. Such slow tempos make you aware of the movements your fingers have to make to get from note to note, or from chord to chord.

Tone

For advanced players, practicing a piece really slowly is also a good way to work on their tone, and to get the smallest nuances of a piece right: dynamics, intonation, phrasing, and everything else beyond hitting the right notes at the right time.

TIP

A NEW PIECE

There are also various practicing techniques for handling new pieces. As mentioned before, a piece can be divided up into four bar, eight bar, or longer sections, revising the previous sections (and playing them absolutely correctly) before moving on. This is just one of many approaches, and all of these approaches can be mixed to come up with a combination that is most effective for you.

177

Challenge

Starting a new piece is a positive challenge to some, while it makes others feel as if they have to start all over again. Of course, avoiding new pieces will yield no progress. Also, learning to tackle new pieces can help you tackle other problems and deal with new, complex subjects as well — which is just one of the reasons that music students perform better in various academic fields. Some of the tips below apply to more advanced musicians only; others work for beginners too.

Listen

As said before, it is essential that you practice a piece playing only the correct notes. It helps if you can first listen to a recorded version of the new piece so you know what it's supposed to sound like before attempting to play it. Of course, you can also ask your teacher to play the piece for you.

Read along

Reading along while listening to a new piece helps you link the notes to the music. With complex pieces, study the part visually before listening to it, so you won't be surprised by repeats and other markings. Reading the music before playing it also gives you the opportunity to check out all dynamic signs and tempo markings, to locate accidentals (flats, sharps, naturals), and numerous other details and characteristics of the piece — and you don't have to worry about playing the instrument at the same time you're reading.

More

If you have a teacher, ask him or her to tell you about the new piece of music: its general character, its form (12-bar blues or 32-bar AABA? Rondo or suite?), the style, the composer, the era in which it was written, and so on. After all, there's more to music than simply executing the composer's notes.

Step by step

Beginning players are often advised to approach a new piece step by step. First, clap the rhythm of the notes, counting aloud as you go. When you've got the rhythm down, play the melody without

178

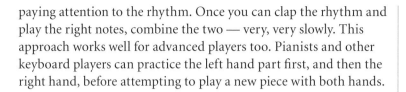

paying attention to the rhythm. Once you can clap the rhythm and play the right notes, combine the two — very, very slowly. This approach works well for advanced players too. Pianists and other keyboard players can practice the left hand part first, and then the right hand, before attempting to play a new piece with both hands.

The trouble spots

Alternatively, depending on your ability and the complexity of the piece, you can play the piece through at an easy tempo, spotting the difficult bits as you go. Playing a piece as such, with mistakes and all, may give you a general idea of what it is about (assuming you haven't heard it before). Other players rather start by locating the tricky bits and figure them out first. A tip: If you're working on a tricky section, always include a few notes or bars before and after that particular section in order to make the tricky section a part of the whole thing, rather than an isolated hurdle that might scare you off every time you see it coming.

Analyzing the trouble spots

If you're having a problem with a certain section, you can simply play it again and again (and again) until you get it right. However, it might be more effective to find out what's causing the problem in the first place. Is it the fingering (which fingers to use for which note)? The rhythm? Or can you not play the part with your left hand while your right hand is doing something else? Or is it a note higher or lower than you can play or sing? Without proper answers to those questions, it will be hard to move on — and before you get to the answers, you need to come up with the right questions. Again, this is something a teacher may be able to help you with. One step beyond analyzing the trouble spots is developing exercises that help the student tackle them. This is something advanced players do for themselves, and something that teachers should teach their students.

MEMORIZING MUSIC

Opinions differ as to whether you should memorize music. Some teachers insist that you should; others feel that memorizing music should be optional, unless you're considering a professional career in music.

Why?
Why would you learn to memorize a piece that can simply read?

- It can help make you **a better musician**. If you don't have to focus on reading, you can fully focus on other elements — tone, phrasing, dynamics, and so on — and listen to yourself play. Also, to play from memory you have to really know a piece inside out, which can only help improve your performance.

- **It makes you look good**. Professional soloists play without sheet music, so why can't you?

- On some instruments, playing by heart allows you to **watch your hands** as you play. Not a very professional approach, but it can be handy.

Why not?
Of course, there's no need to keep musicians from memorizing music (and some are extremely good at it), but why force them?

- Being required to play without sheet music makes a performance an **even more stressful** event — and wasn't making music about enjoying yourself?

- Worrying about what'll happen if you **forget the piece** does not inspire a good performance. It takes away more energy from the music than reading notes does. In other words, some just need sheet music to play well, even while others might play better without it.

- If you're **not good at memorizing music**, learning pieces by heart may take up valuable time that's probably better spent on things you can do to grow musically. Do note that learning to memorize music takes time too: It's not something you just can do.

Techniques and tips

There are various ways and techniques to memorize music. What works great for you, may not work for your friend, and vice versa. The following shortlist helps you recognize how typically handle things, and offers some suggestions.

- You can memorize a piece as you learn it, or you can wait to memorize it once you can play it correctly.

- Memorize **small sections** at a time. For some, a small section is one or two bars; for others, it's half a page. Start with the first section, and add subsequent sections only after you've mastered previous sections.

- Some memorize **the difficult parts** first, repeating them so often that they become as easy to play as the rest of the piece. Only after mastering the difficult parts do they include the other sections. *Tip:* Many teachers claim that you should never play a piece in any other order than the one intended.

- Most musicians memorize a piece **from beginning to the end**, but there are those who prefer to do it the other way around, working their way back to the beginning.

- You can also memorize bits and pieces **as you go**. Try not to look at the music while you're playing, glancing up only as you feel you need to. Bit by bit, over time, you will learn to play the entire piece by heart.

- If you **repeat a piece** or a section over and over, you're using your finger memory or tactile memory. Your fingers know what to do because they've been trained to execute the patterns that are required for that piece of music. It's a relatively easy way to memorize, but it's not very reliable. Changing the tempo of the piece may confuse you (or your fingers). If you want to know if you've really memorized the music, play it at an extremely slow tempo and see what happens.

- Alternatively, you can analyze the piece **step by step**, studying every single aspect of it. This requires a lot of knowledge (scales, harmony, etcetera), but it's the most reliable way to memorize.

- Practicing a piece **away from your instrument** may help you

181

memorize it. Just play it in your imagination, first with, then without the music. This is referred to as shadow practicing or armchair memorizing. You can also try to hear the piece in your head without playing it, before you go to sleep, or on your way to work. Or sing it while you're taking a shower.

- It also helps if you make up **a story that fits the music**!

- **Slow practicing** is good for memorizing music.

- And when you're almost done, **put the book away**. Don't leave it on the music stand, pretending or trying not to peek, but put it in the other room. Out of sight, out of mind? Then try again.

16

Being Prepared

A dry throat, butterflies in your stomach, jitters and shakes, weak knees, trembling fingers, a throbbing heart... All familiar sensations to most anyone who ever climbed a stage to perform, audition, or take a music exam (and those who claim they've never experienced such symptoms are often said to be lying or dead!)

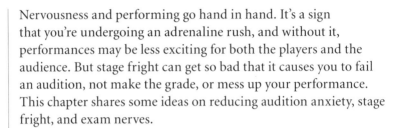

Nervousness and performing go hand in hand. It's a sign that you're undergoing an adrenaline rush, and without it, performances may be less exciting for both the players and the audience. But stage fright can get so bad that it causes you to fail an audition, not make the grade, or mess up your performance. This chapter shares some ideas on reducing audition anxiety, stage fright, and exam nerves.

Books
Many books have been written on this subject, and there is a whole lot more to be said and taught about it. The tips in this chapter touch the mere basics; and as obvious as they seem, they're often quite effective.

Adults and kids
Kids seem to suffer less from jitters and other anxiety symptoms than most teens and adults. So one of the best ways to prevent such feelings in the first place is to begin performing in public at an early age, be it with a school band, playing mini-recitals for the family every week or after each practice session — even if it's only briefly. As taking this advice may not be an option if you're already beyond early childhood, keep on reading.

PREPARING YOURSELF

First, a look at what could, or should, be done beforehand.

Practice, practice, practice
If you're not fully prepared for a performance, an audition, or a music exam, you have every reason to be nervous. Practicing efficiently, possibly under the guidance of a teacher, is one key to abating performance anxiety. A tip: The closer the time of the main event comes, the more important it is to focus practice sessions on problem areas, rather than on playing known material. A rule of thumb is to be able to play the tricky bits at least five to ten times in a row without stumbling. Only then can you be sure

184

that you've got them down. *Tip:* Make yourself start over from the beginning after each mistake, even if it's the very last note. This can make playing the final run almost as thrilling as an audition.

> ### Too late
> If you feel that you have to spend hours practicing the day before the performance, or on the actual day, you probably failed to use your previous practice sessions to the fullest.

TIP

Slips
Even professionals make mistakes, so preparing a piece includes preparing for stumbles and slips. Practice how to recover quickly and continue to play in the correct tempo. You can learn how to deal with slip-ups. One simple tip: do not make a face as this will just draw everyone's attention to your mistake. Note that there are music teachers who specialize in audition preparation!

Memory
You may play from memory to impress the jury or the members of the band, but consider bringing your sheet music along if memorization was not required. Having it there will make it easier to start over if you do slip. Does your piece require page turning? Then it would be helpful to memorize the first section on the following page. Another tip for auditions or exams: Make sure you make a list of the pieces you're going to play and bring it with you. It really doesn't look good if you've forgotten the title of your next piece.

Accompanist
If you're going to play with an accompanist during the performance, it's best if that's the person you rehearse with as well. Playing with a stranger can cause added tension, and a familiar face can be a great confidence booster. Even if not required, you may want to consider doing your piece with accompaniment (if you're not already the pianist or guitarist): Having another person there may help reduce stress, and it usually makes for a more entertaining performance too.

185

Deal with it

No matter how well-prepared you are, exams, auditions, and performances will induce stress and nervousness. Dealing with this is part of the learning process of playing, period. Practice doesn't make perfect, but the more you play (and the more exams or auditions you do), the better you will eventually become at handling stage fright.

Surrender

Fighting your nerves is not a good idea either. Doing so can even add to your stress level, which is probably already substantial. Telling yourself to be calm usually doesn't work either. You aren't calm, so it's actually better to just surrender to that. The fact that your nerves can make your performance less than brilliant just shows how important it is to be well-prepared.

Mock auditions

The more used to playing for an audience you are, the less likely you are to be nervous for auditions or exams. Still, these situations are different from regular performances: They occur less frequently and there's usually a lot riding on them. A mistake made during a performance typically has fewer consequences than a slip at an audition. Staging mock auditions (a.k.a. placebo auditions or dress rehearsals) often helps in getting used to the extra tension. They can take place at home, while playing for family and friends. Some teachers organize mock auditions too. *Tip:* Turn mock auditions into a complete performance, including a formal entrance into the room, presenting yourself, and so on. Also, ask your audience to evaluate your playing afterwards to ensure that they were attentive to every note you played. Scary? That's the idea.

Recording in advance

Recording the pieces you'll be playing at the audition or exam can by very effective. First, a recording allows you to listen and evaluate your performance, as it's very difficult to do that while you're playing. And the recorded results can give you the objectivity you need to really assess what you're doing. Second, a simple recording device can have the same effect as an attentive audience in that it can make you nervous enough to perhaps make the kind of mistakes you would in front of a real audience. Getting used to the presence of a recording device is quite similar to getting used to an audience, so that makes it effective training.

Evaluate the recording

Don't forget to evaluate the recording, and don't listen for mistakes only. Pay close attention to timing, intonation, dynamics, and all other elements that make for a great performance, including tone. Evaluating the latter requires good recording and playback equipment. *Tip:* First warm up, and then try to play your prepared pieces and scales right during the first take — just like in real life!

Presentation

Are you required or do you want to dress a certain way for the performance? Then decide beforehand what you're going to wear, how to wear your hair, etcetera. Don't wait until the day of the show to do this, but get your look together at least the day before.

Sleep

And don't forget: A good night's sleep, or a nap before an afternoon performance, often works wonders!

SHOW TIME

There are many remedies for reducing nerves on the day of your performance too. First of all, leave home early so there's no need to rush, and make sure there's plenty of time to prepare for the performance once you're on site.

Relax

For some, simply repeating the words, 'I'm calm, I'm cool,' is enough to help them relax, but most people need more than

187

this. There are many different techniques, ranging from deep-breathing exercises to meditation, yoga, or special methods like the Alexander Technique or neurofeedback. You may also benefit from simple stretching, jumping, and other physical movement, and for some, screaming helps.

Transfer your stress
Another idea is to find a physical release for your stress. For example, take a paperclip along and hold it when you feel nervous, imagining that all of your extra energy is being drawn through your hand into the paperclip — then throw it away before you go onstage.

Warming-up
Warm-up routines (long notes, scales, and so on) not only get you musically prepared to perform, they can also help you relax. Long, slow notes are more effective than up-tempo riffs, obviously. If you feel the need to go through your scales and prepared pieces once more, you probably aren't really ready. *Tip:* Find a quiet place to prepare, if possible.

Silence
If there's no opportunity to actually play before you go onstage, just moving your fingers over the keys or the strings of your instrument will help. Wind instrument players can warm up their instrument by blowing warm air through it.

The instrument
Make sure the instrument is in good repair, and thoroughly check it before the performance. Exam judges may forgive a broken string, a failed reed, or a stuck valve, but even so, these things won't promote a confident performance. Brasswind players: If you've warmed up to prepare for your performance, make sure to drain your horn before going onstage.

Tuning and warming-up
Tuning the instrument under the observant eyes of your audience, the jurors, or the examiners may be nerve-wracking, so make sure you take care of this in advance, if possible.

Imagine

Many musicians fight their nerves by conjuring calming imagery. They imagine playing at home or on their favorite stage rather than in front of a jury; or they concentrate on a recent holiday, or pretend they're on a deserted island. Others promise themselves that this is their very last performance ever, so they need to give it all — now or never.

Pep talk

Giving yourself a pep talk may help too. But rather than just telling yourself to be cool and calm, tell yourself that you wouldn't even be here if your teacher hadn't thought you were ready — you've earned your way there.

Focus

Don't focus on the outcome of the audition or exam. Instead, concentrate on your music, as that's really what it's all about. What may also help is to make your objective the demonstration of the beauty of the music you're going to play, rather than how impressive a player you are.

Smile

Smile when you enter the room. It will make you both look and feel better. Stand up straight and put both feet firmly on the floor. It helps, really.

A different type of audience

Auditioners and examiners are a particular kind of audience. They're there to judge your playing, rather than just enjoy the music. Still, it's good to realize that they're there for you; know that they want you to play your best and to make you feel at ease.

Any audience

It may help to calm you if you look at your examiners and auditioners the same way you'd look at a 'regular' audience: Tell yourself that they're all very kind people (which they usually are, so this shouldn't be too hard). Make eye contact with your jurors just as you would any other audience, and smile. And just as you might focus on the people you know, or the ones responding

189

favorably to you in a regular performance, focus on the juror who smiles back at you.

> ### Imagine
> *Another approach is to completely ignore the audience (imagine that you're playing at home alone); but realize that this might not work at an audition or an exam. A popular method is to imagine the audience (large or small, jurors or not) sitting in their underwear, feeling even more uncomfortable than you are onstage. Or think of the audience as non-musicians who will be impressed by every single note you play, or as the ultimate experts who showed up just to hear you play!*

The first note

Take a couple of seconds before you start playing. Breathe. Get the tempo of the piece going in your head, or even sing the first few bars in your mind; imagine yourself playing the song. Then it's time for the first note. Make it sound great, and enjoy your performance!

AND MORE

If none of the above works for you, try consulting one of the many books on the subject. Another option is to take a yoga or meditation course, for example, or consider a drama class.

Food and drinks

Various types of food and drink are said to make anxiety worse (e.g., coffee, tea, and other products with caffeine, sugar, or salt), while others help to soothe your nerves. Bananas contain potassium, which helps you relax, and there are various types of calming herbal teas, for example. Alcohol may make you feel

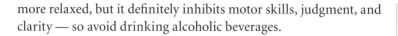

more relaxed, but it definitely inhibits motor skills, judgment, and clarity — so avoid drinking alcoholic beverages.

Drugs

Many professional musicians take beta blockers (heart medication, actually) to combat their performance anxiety. This type of drug is considered relatively safe, and it works a lot faster than a yoga course and most other relaxation techniques. But you should wonder if music is your thing if you need drugs to do it, even if it's only for high-stress situations, like an audition. Try instead to reduce, if not eliminate, stressors; only do things that make you feel good, and avoid those that induce anxiety. Music is supposed to be fun!

Chapters 15 and 16 were taken from Tipbook Music for Kids and Teens *(see page 225) and adapted for* Tipbook Trumpet and Trombone.

Tipcode List

The Tipcodes in this book offer easy access to short videos, sound files, and other additional information at www.tipbook.com. For your convenience, the Tipcodes in this Tipbook have been listed below.

Tipcode	Topic	Chapter	Page
TRP-002	Trumpet and flugelhorn	1	2
TRP-003	Harmonics	2	6
TRP-004	Second valve	2	8
TRP-005	Trigger	2	14
TRP-007	Depressing a valve	5	58
TRP-008	Testing hand slide	5	75
TRP-009	Straight mute	7	96
TRP-010	Cup mute	7	96
TRP-011	Harmon mute	7	97
TRP-012	Plunger	7	98
TRP-013	Assembling a trombone	8	102
TRP-014	A=440	8	106
TRP-015	Tuning fork	8	106
TRP-016	Tuning (tuning slide)	8	107
TRP-017	440 vs 442	8	109
TRP-018	Lubricating a rotor	9	125
TRP-019	Removing valve slide with cloth	9	131
TRP-020	How they're made	12	149

Glossary

This glossary briefly explains most of the jargon touched on so far. It also contains some terms that haven't been mentioned yet, but which you may come across in other books, in magazines, or online. Most terms are explained in more detail as they are introduced in this book. Please consult the index on pages 220–222.

Alto trombone
Higher pitched, smaller trombone
in E–flat.

American cornet
The American cornet is longer than
the British or European cornet.

Bach trumpet
See: *Piccolo trumpet.*

Backbore
See: *Mouthpiece.*

Background brass
Generally low-pitched brass instruments that are mostly used to
accompany the melody instruments.
Examples are euphoniums, mellophones, baritones, and alto horns.
See also: *Soprano brass.*

Bass trombone
The bass trombone basically has the
same dimensions as a tenor trombone, but with an extra large bore
and bell. Most instruments come
with two valves.

Bell, bell section
The material and taper of the bell
section are important to the sound.
Some trumpets have a tunable bell.

Bell stay
The brace in the bell section of a
trombone.

B♭ instruments
The most widely-used trumpet is the
B♭ trumpet. If you play a C, you will
hear a concert B♭. Most cornets and
flugelhorns are B♭ instruments too,
but these *transposing instruments*
come in other keys as well. Tenor
trombones, though pitched in B♭

as well, are usually not considered
transposing instruments.

Booster
Metal cap that adds weight to your
mouthpiece.

Bore
The bore refers to the size or shape
of the inside of a tube. A wide tube
has a large bore, a narrow tube has
a small bore. A straight tube has
a *cylindrical bore*, a tube that gets
steadily wider has a *conical bore*. A
trombone is largely cylindrical, a
flugelhorn is largely conical.

Bottom spring, bottom-sprung
See: *Top spring, top-sprung.*

Brass
An alloy made of copper and zinc;
the material most commonly used
for brass instruments.

British cornet
See: *American cornet.*

Bugle
One of the *natural instruments*, a
bugle is like a flugelhorn without
valves.

Conical
See: *Bore.*

Convertible trombone
A trombone with a detachable F-
attachment. See also: *F-attachment.*

Cornet, Cornet à pistons
Cornet à pistons or even *piston* is
an older name for the short, British
cornet.

194

Crook
See: *Tuning slide.*

C–trumpet
Slightly smaller than the 'regular' B♭ trumpet. See: *B♭ instrument.*

Cup
The cup–shaped part of the mouth-piece, within which your lips vibrate.

Cylinder, cylinder valve
See: *Valve.*

Cylindrical
See: *Bore.*

Dual bore
A dual bore trombone has a slide with two different bores. Some trumpets come with a dual bore too.

Embouchure
Your embouchure or 'lip' is your way of playing and your use of lips, jaws and all the muscles around them.

F–attachment
A tube and valve assembly that lowers the pitch of a trombone by a fourth.

Finger buttons
You operate the valves with the finger buttons.

Fluegelhorn
Alternative spelling for flugelhorn.

French style slides
Vertical valve slides, as used on most flugelhorns.

German trumpet
See: *Valves.*

Gig bag
Reinforced bag.

Gooseneck
The first piece of tubing of a trombone's bell section.

Handgrip
The inner- slide brace or inner brace on a trombone.

Harmonic
The notes you can play without us-ing the valves are called harmonics. *Natural instruments* have no valves and can play only harmonics.

Independent, in-line
On bass-trombones with in-line or independent rotary valves, the valves can be used independently from each other. If the valves are *stacked* or *offset*, they can't.

Inner slide, outer slide
See: *Slide.*

Intonation
The better the intonation of an instrument, the easier it is to play it in tune.

Jazz trombone
Another word for valve trombone, i.e., a trombone with valves instead of a slide.

Lacquer
Most modern brass instruments are lacquered. Some are silver- or gold-plated instead. Occasionally, you will find nickel-plated instruments too. See also: *Plating.*

Lapping
Polishing parts for a perfect fit.

195

Leadpipe
Also called *mouthpipe*: the piece
of tubing between the mouthpiece
receiver and the tuning slide.

Lip
See: *Embouchure*.

Low brass
Low brass includes lower pitched
instruments such as baritones and
tubas.

Lyre, lyre holder
Holder of marching size sheet music.

Main tuning slide
See: *Tuning slide*.

Monel
Copper/nickel alloy, often used for
valves.

Mouthpiece
Important for your technique and
how comfortably you play. Dimensions to take into account are: the
size and depth of the *cup*, the width
and shape of the *rim*, the smallest
opening (*bore* or *throat*) and the
shape and size of the *backbore* (the
inside of the *shank*, the part of the
mouthpiece that fits into the mouthpiece receiver of your instrument.

Mouthpiece receiver
See: *Receiver*.

Mouthpipe
See: *Leadpipe*.

Mute
Mutes allow you to create all kinds
of special effects and timbres. Prac-

tice mutes are the only type of mute
that effectively *mutes* the sound.

Natural instrument
Natural instruments have no valves
and can only play harmonics. They
are also known as *signal instruments*.
See also: *Harmonic*.

Nickel silver
Alloy of copper, zinc, nickel, and
some other metals — but no silver.
Also known as German silver, white
bronze or alpaca.

Offset
See: *Independent, in-line*.

Outer slide, inner slide
See: *Slide*.

Périnet valves
See: *Valves*.

Piccolo trumpet
Small, very high-sounding trumpet
with four valves. Also called *Bach
trumpet*.

Piston, piston valves
See: *Valves*.

Piston guides
Guide that makes for accurate port
alignment. Also known as valve
guides.

Plating
Instead of lacquer, an instrument may be silver-plated or even
gold-plated. These precious metals
will last longer than lacquer will.
Virtually all mouthpieces are silver-
plated, but gold-plated mouthpieces
are also available.

196

Pocket trumpet
Very tightly 'rolled-up' trumpet; sounds the same pitch as a regular trumpet.

Practice mute
A type of mute that greatly reduces the volume of your instrument.

Receiver
The tube you stick your mouthpiece into. Also called *Venturi tube*.

Reversed leadpipe, reversed tuning slide
The tuning slide slides over the leadpipe, rather than into it, creating a smoother airflow.

Rim
The rim of the mouthpiece (see: *Mouthpiece*) or the edge of the bell.

Rotary instrument
Instrument with *rotary valves* or *rotors*. See: *Valves.*

Rotary valve, rotor
See: *Valves.*

Shank
See: *Mouthpiece.*

Shepherd's crook
On the short, British cornet, the double bend after the valves has the shape of a shepherd's crook.

Slide
The slide or *hand slide* of a trombone consists of an *inner slide* (with two tubes) and a moveable *outer slide*. You hold the *inner slide* with the *inner slide brace* or inner brace and you work the outer slide with the *outer brace* or *slide stay*. At the two ends,

the inner tube gets slightly thicker. These thickened ends are referred to as the *stockings*. See also: *Valve slides.*

Slide lock
Stops a trombone slide moving of its own accord.

Slide stop
Prevents a (third) valve slide from slipping off.

Slide trumpet
Old-fashioned trumpet; incorrect name for the trombone.

Soprano brass
Brass instruments can be divided in soprano brass, which includes the higher sounding horns (trumpets, cornets, etc.), and low brass (trombone, tuba, euphonium, etc.). See also: *Background brass.*

Spit valve
See: *Water key.*

Stacked
See: *Independent, in-line.*

Stockings
Thicker sections at the ends of a trombone slide's inner tubes.

Straight bore
See: *Dual bore.*

Straight trombone
Trombone without an (F) attachment.

Tenor trombone
The most popular trombone; comes with or without F-attachment. See also: *F-attachment.*

Throat
See: *Mouthpiece.*

Top action, top spring
On most piston-type valves, the spring is above the piston (*top action* or *top spring*). On a bottom-sprung valve it is underneath the piston.

Transposing instruments
See: *B♭ instruments.*

Trigger
Mechanism to operate the valve slide(s) on a flugelhorn. Sometimes used on trumpets and cornets too.

Trim
Replaceable parts, i.e., valve stems, finger buttons, valve caps, etc.

Tuning bell, tunable bell
See: *Bell.*

Tuning crook
See: *Tuning slide.*

Tuning slide
You tune a flugelhorn with the tuning slide, the (straight) section of tubing into which the mouthpiece fits. Trumpets, cornets and trombones are tuned with the U-shaped tuning slide or main tuning slide, also known as (main) tuning crook.

Valves
Valves are used to make the tube of an instrument longer, lowering the tones it can produce. Most trumpets, cornets, and flugelhorns have piston valves or Périnet valves that work with a piston, moving up and down.

The main part of a rotary valve, rotor, or cylinder valve, which can be found on trombones and rotary trumpets (a.k.a. German trumpets), among other horns, makes a rotating movement. The group of valves on an instrument is referred to as valve section, valve cluster, or valve block.

Valve casing
Each piston is enclosed in its own valve casing.

Valve guide
See: *Piston guide.*

Valve slides
U-shaped pieces of tubing attached to the valves; also referred to as slides.

Valve trombone
Trombone with piston valves and no slide, like a trumpet. Also known as valved trombone.

Venturi tube
See: *Receiver.*

Water key
Water keys allow you to remove the condensation that collects in your instrument. They're also known as spit valves.

Wrap
Trombones with one or two valves may have an open wrap, with the extra tubing of the attachment(s) sticking out behind the instrument, or a closed or traditional wrap, where it stays within the bell section. See also: *F-attachment.*

Want to Know More?

Tipbooks supply you with basic information on the instrument of your choice, and everything that comes with it. Of course there's a lot more to be found on all of the subjects you came across on these pages. This section offers a selection of magazines, books, helpful websites, and more.

MAGAZINES
This list includes the main magazines for brass players.

- *Brass Band World* (UK), www.brassbandworld.com

- *Brass Bulletin* (online magazine), www.brass-bulletin.ch

- *British Bandsman* (UK; weekly), www.britishbandsman.com

- *ITG Journal*, www.trumpetguild.org (published by the ITG, International Trumpet Guild)

- *The Brass Herald* (UK), www.thebrassherald.com

- *The Brass Player*, www.charlescolin.com/nybc/bp.htm

- *Windplayer*, www.windplayer.com

BOOKS
The following is a brief selection of brasswind books that cover some of the subjects of this Tipbook in greater depth.

- *20th Century Brass Musical Instruments in the United States*, by Richard J. Dundas (Honeybee Health Products, 1998; 88 pages; ISBN 978-0961709310).

- *A Complete Guide to Brass Instruments and Techniques*, by Scott Whitener (Schirmer Books, 2006; 432 pages; ISBN 978-0534509880).

- *Brass Instruments: Their History and Development*, by Anthony Baines (Dover Publications, 1993; 300 pages; ISBN 978-0486275741).

- *Musical Wind Instruments*, by Adam von Ahn Carse (Courier Dover Publications, 2002, 416 pages, ISBN 978-0486424224).

- *Sound the Trumpet: How to Blow Your Own Horn*, by Jonathan Harnum (Sol Ut Press, 2006; 320 pages; ISBN 978-0970751270).

- *The Cambridge Companion to Brass Instruments*, edited by Trevor Herbert and John Wallace (Cambridge University Press, 1997; 325 pages; ISBN 978-0521565226).

- *The Sax & Brass Book: Saxophones, Trumpets and Trombones in Jazz, Rock and Pop*, by Tony Bacon (Backbeat Books, 2003; 120 pages; ISBN 978-0879307370).

- *The Trombone* (Yale Musical Instrument Series), by Trevor Herbert (Yale University Press, 2006; 336 pages; ISBN 978-0300100952).

- *The Trombonist's Handbook: a Complete Guide to Playing and Teaching the Trombone*, by Reginald H. Fink (Accura Music, Ohio, 1977; 145 pages; ISBN 0 918194 01 6).

- *Trombone: Its History and Music*, 1697-1811, by D.M. Guion (Routledge, 1988; 344 pages; ISBN 978-2881242113).

- *Trumpet & Trombone*, by Bate Philip (W. W. Norton and Company, Inc., 1980; 324 pages; ISBN 978-0393336016)

ONLINE

There is a lot of information on brass instruments available online. Do check out the websites of brass instrument makers, as well as non-commercial websites such as:

- Bass Trombone Info: www.basstrombone.info

- Brass Resources: www.whc.net/rjones/brassrsc.html

- British Trombone Society: www.britishtrombonesociety.org

- David Wilkin brass resources: facstaff.unca.edu/dwilken/brassresources.html

- Jazz Trombone FAQ: www.geocities.com/bourbonstreet/2418/faq.html

- Online Trombone Journal: www.trombone.org

- Proprietary Serial Number Lists: www.musictrader.com/serialnos.html

- The Trumpet Herald: www.trumpetherald.com (forum)

- Trombone Page Of The World: www.trombone-usa.com

- Trumpet Master: www.trumpetmaster.com (forum)

- Trumpet Player Online: www.trumpetplayeronline.com

- Trumpet Players' International Network: www.tpin.org

BRASSWIND ORGANIZATIONS

There are many organizations that aim to promote the practice and performance of brass music, and to assist brass music artists and students. The following list is not intended to be complete.

- International Trombone Association (ITA): www.ita-web.org
- International Trumpet Guild (ITG): www.trumpetguild.org
- North American Brass Band Association: www.nabba.org
- American Brass Chamber Music Association Inc.: www.americanbrassquintet.org/ABCMA.html
- British Federation of Brass Bands: www.bfbb.co.uk
- European Brass Band Association: www.ebba.eu.com
- National Band Council of Australia: www.nbca.asn.au
- Brass Bands' Association of New Zealand: www.brassnz.co.nz
- Irish Association of Brass and Concert Bands: www.iabcb.ie
- Scottish Brass Band Association: www.sbba.org.uk

LOOKING FOR A TEACHER?

If you want to find a teacher online, try searching for "trumpet teacher" or "trombone teacher" and the name of the area or city where you live, or visit one of the following special interest websites:

- PrivateLessons.com: www.privatelessons.com
- MusicStaff.com: www.musicstaff.com
- The Music Teachers List: www.teachlist.com

Trumpet Fingering
Charts

There are various ways to present fingering charts for trumpet, cornet, and flugelhorn players.

First, the entire range of the trumpet is printed, showing which valves to press for each note. Alternate fingerings are included where relevant. In a second series of diagrams, you can see which notes you can play with each valve combination (see page page2 208–210).

Alternate fingerings

Various notes can be played using one or more alternate fingerings. Some of these fingerings may sound less (or more, depending on your instrument) in tune than the standard fingerings. Try them out and see how they sound on your horn!

1+2=3

Using the first and second valves lowers the fundamental pitch with three half steps, and so does pressing the third valve (see pages 8–9). In practice, however, most players always use 1+2 rather than 3. This combination is usually easier to play and typically more in tune.

Valve slides

Some notes need to be adjusted, such as low D and D♭, which are sharp by nature. Depending on the fingering, you can use your third or first valve slide to adjust such notes. See pages 54–56 for more information on this subject.

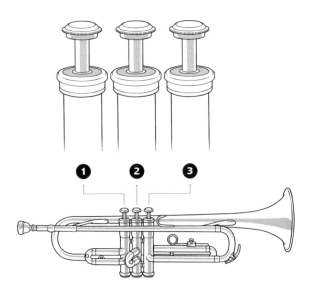

F♯3 – G♭3

① ② ③

G3

① ② ③

G♯3 – A♭3

① ② ③

A3

① ② ③

Alternate:

① ② ③

A♯3 – B♭3

① ② ③

B3 – C♭4

① ② ③

C4 – B♯3

① ② ③

C♯4 – D♭4

① ② ③

D4

① ② ③

D♯4 – E♭4

① ② ③

E4 – F♭4

① ② ③

Alternate:

① ② ③

F4 – E♯4

① ② ③

205

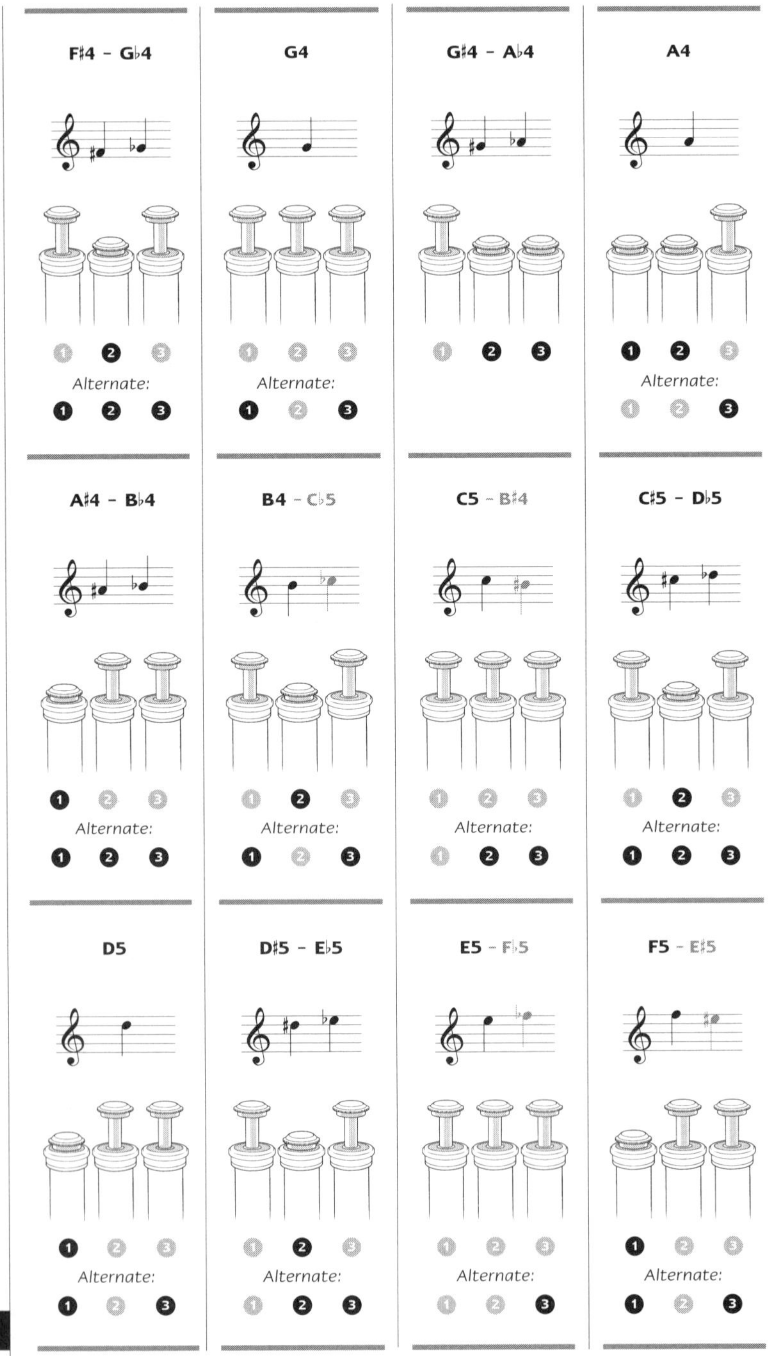

F♯4 – G♭4

G4

G♯4 – A♭4

A4

A♯4 – B♭4

B4 – C♭5

C5 – B♯4

C♯5 – D♭5

D5

D♯5 – E♭5

E5 – F♭5

F5 – E♯5

F♯5 – G♭5

Alternate:

G5

Alternate:

G♯5 – A♭5

Alternate:

A5

Alternate:

A♯5 – B♭5

Alternate:

B5 – C♭6

Alternate:

C6 – B♯5

Alternate:

C♯6 – D♭6

Alternate:

D6

Alternate:

D♯6 – E♭6

Alternate:

E6 – F♭6

Alternate:

F6 – E♯6

Alternate:

207

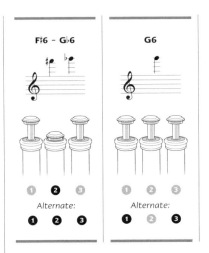

Valve combinations

Instead of looking at all the notes of the trumpet range and how to play them, you can also take a look at the various valve combinations and the notes they allow you to play.

1ˢᵗ position

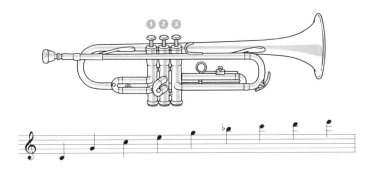

2ⁿᵈ position

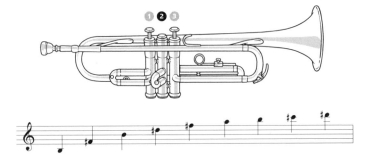

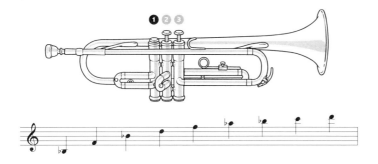

3rd position

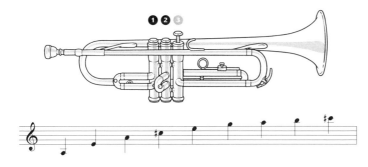

4th position (1+2)

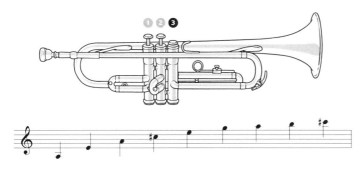

4st position (3)

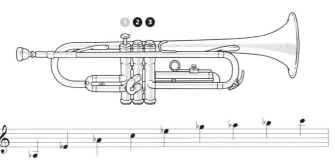

5th position

6th position

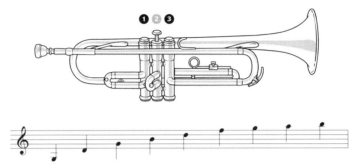

7th position

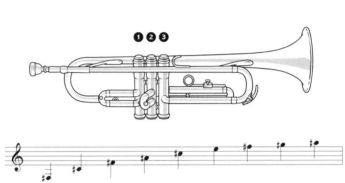

Trombone Slide
Position Charts

Just like trumpet fingering charts, trombone slide position charts can be presented in different ways.

First, the trombone slide positions are listed by showing the correct slide position for each note. Some notes can be played in various positions, as you will see.

F attachment

An F attachment not only allows you to play a number of additional pitches; it also increases the number of usable slide positions on your instruments! These extra positions are shown as well.

F-attachment

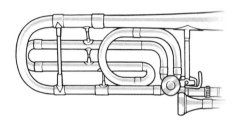

Pitch adjustment

On the trombone, some notes tend to be flat (too low) or sharp (too high), even if you play the finest of instruments. For example, F3, F4, and F5 tend to be sharp. To play these notes in tune, you simply need to extend your slide a bit more. D4 tends to be flat, so you move your slide in untill it sounds you hear the correct pitch. On the following pages, arrows indicate these slide adjustments.

Slide positions (straight trombone)

Slide positions with F-attach-ment; lever depressend.

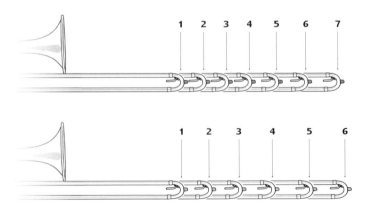

C2 – B♯2	D♭2 – C♯2	D2	E♭2 – D♯2
slide position	slide position	slide position	slide position
F-att. only: **6**	F-att. only: **5**	F-att. only: **4**	F-att. only: **3**

E2 – F♭2	F2 – E♯2	F♯2 – G♭2	G2
slide position	slide position	slide position	slide position
7	**6**	**5**	**4**
with F-att.: **2**	with F-att.: **1**		

A♭2 – G♯2	A2	B♭2 – A♯2	B2 – C♭3
slide position	slide position	slide position	slide position
3	**2**	**1**	**7**
		with F-att.: **3**	with F-att.: **2**

C3 – B♯2	D♭3 – C♯3	D3	E♭3 – D♯
slide position	slide position	slide position	slide position
6	**5**	**4**	**3**
with F-att.: **1**			

E3 – F♭3	F3 – E♯3	F♯3 – G♭3	G3
slide position	slide position	slide position	slide position
7	**6**	**5**	**4**

213

A♭3 – G♯3	A3	B♭3 – A♯3	B3 – C♭4
slide position **3**	slide position **2**	slide position **1 or 5**	slide position **4**

C4 – B♯3	D♭4 – C♯4	D4	E♭4 – D♯4
slide position **3**	slide position **2**	slide position **1 or 4**	slide position **3**

E4 – F♭4	F4 – E♯4	F♯4 – G♭4	G4
slide position **2**	slide position **1 or 4**	slide position **3**	slide position **2**

A♭4 – G♯4	A4	B♭4 – A♯4	B4 – C♭4
slide position **3**	slide position **2**	slide position **1**	slide position **1**

C5 – B♯4	C♯5 – D♭5	D5	
slide position **3**	slide position **2**	slide position **1**	

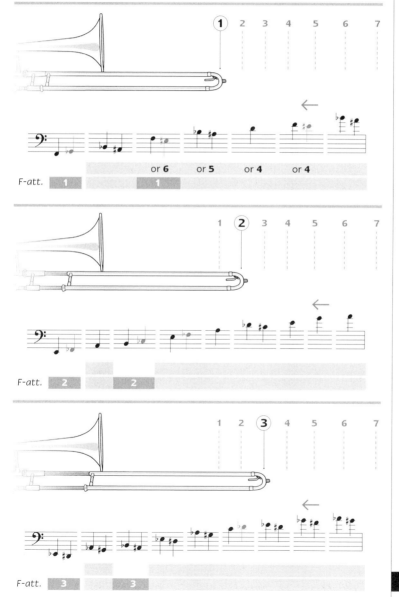

Notes per position

Rather than showing the notes to play and their slide positions, you can also list the slide positions and add the notes they allow you to play. Here they are!

← / →
*Adjust
slide position
in/out*

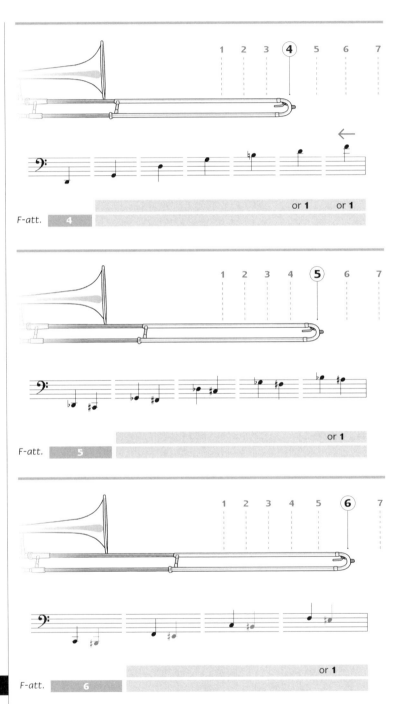

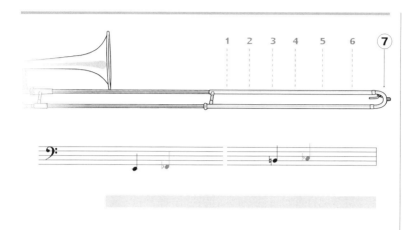

Essential Data

In the event of your instrument being stolen or lost, or if you decide to sell it, it's useful to have all the relevant data at hand. Here are two pages to list everything you need — for the insurance, for the police, or just for yourself.

INSURANCE

Company: _____ Phone: _____

Website: _____ E-mail: _____

Agent: _____

Phone: _____

Website: _____ E-mail: _____

Policy number: _____ Premium: _____

INSTRUMENTS AND ACCESSORIES

Brand and type: _____

Serial number: _____

Price: _____

Date of purchase: _____

Purchased from: _____

Phone: _____ Email: _____

Brand and type: _____

Serial number: _____

Price: _____

Date of purchase: _____

Purchased from: _____

Phone: _____ Email: _____

Brand and type:

Serial number:

Price:

Date of purchase:

Purchased from:

Phone: Email:

Brand and type:

Serial number:

Price:

Date of purchase:

Purchased from:

Phone: Email:

Brand and type:

Serial number:

Price:

Date of purchase:

Purchased from:

Phone: Email:

ADDITIONAL NOTES

Index

Please check the glossary on pages 193–198 for additional definitions of the terms used in this book.

221

Interactive Books with TIPCODES

The Tipbook Series

Did you like this Tipbook? There are also Tipbooks for your fellow band or orchestra members! The Tipbook Series features various books on musical instruments, including the singing voice, in addition to Tipbook Music on Paper, Tipbook Amplifiers and Effects, and Tipbook Music for Kids and Teens – a Guide for Parents.

Every Tipbook is a highly accessible and easy-to-read compilation of the knowledge and expertise of numerous musicians, teachers, technicians, and other experts, written for musicians of all ages, at all levels, and in any style of music. Please check www.tipbook.com for up to date information on the Tipbook Series!

All Tipbooks come with Tipcodes that offer additional information, sound files and short movies at www.tipbook.com.

Instrument Tipbooks

All instrument Tipbooks offer a wealth of highly accessible, yet well-founded information on one or more closely related instruments. The first chapters of each Tipbook explain the very basics of the instrument(s), explaining all the parts and what they do, describing what's involved in learning to play, and indicating typical instrument prices. The core chapters, addressing advanced players as well, turn you into an instant expert on the instrument. This knowledge allows you to make an informed purchase and get the most out of your instrument. Comprehensive chapters on maintenance, intonation, and tuning are also included, as well a brief section on the history, the family, and the production of the instrument.

Tipbook Acoustic Guitar – $14.95

Tipbook Acoustic Guitar explains all of the elements that allow you to recognize and judge a guitar's timbre, performance, and playability, focusing on both steel-string and nylon-string instruments. There are chapters covering the various types of strings and their characteristics, and there's plenty of helpful information on changing and cleaning strings, on tuning and maintenance, and even on the care of your fingernails.

223

Tipbook Amplifiers and Effects – $14.99

Whether you need a guitar amp, a sound system, a multi-effects unit for a bass guitar, or a keyboard amplifier, *Tipbook Amplifiers and Effects* helps you to make a good choice. Two chapters explain general features (controls, equalizers, speakers, MIDI, etc.) and figures (watts, ohms, impedance, etc.), and further chapters cover the specifics of guitar amps, bass amps, keyboard amps, acoustic amps, and sound systems. Effects and effect units are dealt with in detail, and there are also chapters on microphones and pickups, and cables and wireless systems.

Tipbook Cello – $14.95

Cellists can find everything they need to know about their instrument in *Tipbook Cello*. The book gives you tips on how to select an instrument and choose a bow, tells you all about the various types of strings and rosins, and gives you helpful tips on the maintenance and tuning of your instrument. Basic information on electric cellos is included as well!

Tipbook Clarinet – $14.99

Tipbook Clarinet sheds light on every element of this fascinating instrument. The knowledge presented in this guide makes trying out and selecting a clarinet much easier, and it turns you into an instant expert on offset and in-line trill keys, rounded or French-style keys, and all other aspects of the instrument. Special chapters are devoted to reeds (selecting, testing, and adjusting reeds), mouthpieces and ligatures, and maintenance.

Tipbook Electric Guitar and Bass Guitar – $14.95

Electric guitars and bass guitars come in many shapes and sizes. *Tipbook Electric Guitar and Bass Guitar* explains all of their features and characteristics, from neck profiles, frets, and types of wood to different types of pickups, tuning machines, and — of course — strings. Tuning and advanced do-it-yourself intonation techniques are included.

Tipbook Drums – $14.95

A drum is a drum is a drum? Not true — and *Tipbook Drums* tells you all the ins and outs of their differences, from the type of wood to the dimensions of the shell, the shape of the bearing edge, and the drum's hardware. Special chapters discuss selecting drum sticks, drum heads, and cymbals. Tuning and muffling, two techniques a drummer must master to make the instrument sound as good as it can, are covered in detail, providing step-by-step instructions.

Tipbook Flute and Piccolo – $14.99

Flute prices range from a few hundred to fifty thousand dollars and more. *Tipbook Flute and Piccolo* tells you how workmanship, materials, and other elements make for different instruments with vastly different prices, and teaches you how to find the instrument that best suits your or your child's needs. Open-hole or closed-hole keys, a B-foot or a C-foot, split-E or donut, inline or offset G? You'll be able to answer all these questions — and more — after reading this guide.

Tipbook Keyboard and Digital Piano – $14.99

Buying a home keyboard or a digital piano may find you confronted with numerous unfamiliar terms. *Tipbook Keyboard and Digital Piano* explains all of them in a very easy-to-read fashion — from hammer action and non-weighted keys to MIDI, layers and splits, arpeggiators and sequencers, expression pedals and multi-switches, and more, including special chapters on how to judge the instrument's sound, accompaniment systems, and the various types of connections these instruments offer.

Tipbook Music for Kids and Teens – a Guide for Parents – $14.99

How do you inspire children to play music? How do you inspire them to practice? What can you do to help them select an instrument, to reduce stage fright, or to practice effectively? What can you do to make practice fun? How do you reduce sound levels and

225

prevent hearing damage? These and many more questions are dealt with in *Tipbook Music for Kids and Teens – a Guide for Parents and Caregivers*. The book addresses all subjects related to the musical education of children from pre-birth to pre-adulthood.

Tipbook Music on Paper – $14.99

Tipbook Music on Paper – Basic Theory offers everything you need to read and understand the language of music. The book presumes no prior understanding of theory and begins with the basics, explaining standard notation, but moves on to advanced topics such as odd time signatures and transposing music in a fashion that makes things really easy to understand.

Tipbook Piano – $14.99

Choosing a piano becomes a lot easier with the knowledge provided in *Tipbook Piano*, which makes for a better understanding of this complex, expensive instrument without going into too much detail. How to judge and compare piano keyboards and pedals, the influence of the instrument's dimensions, different types of cabinets, how to judge an instrument's timbre, the difference between laminated and solid wood soundboards, accessories, hybrid and digital pianos, and why tuning and regulation are so important: Everything is covered in this handy guide.

Tipbook Saxophone – $14.95

At first glance, all alto saxophones look alike. And all tenor saxophones do too — yet they all play and sound different from each other. *Tipbook Saxophone* discusses the instrument in detail, explaining the key system and the use of additional keys, the different types of pads, corks, and springs, mouthpieces and how they influence timbre and playability, reeds (and how to select and adjust them) and much more. Fingering charts are also included!

226

Tipbook Trumpet and Trombone, Flugelhorn and Cornet – $14.99

The Tipbook on brass instruments focuses on the smaller horns listed in the title. It explains all of the jargon you come across when you're out to buy or rent an instrument, from bell material to the shape of the bore, the leadpipe, valves and valve slides, and all other elements of the horn. Mouthpieces, a crucial choice for the sound and playability of all brasswinds, are covered in a separate chapter.

Tipbook Violin and Viola – $14.95

Tipbook Violin and Viola covers a wide range of subjects, ranging from an explanation of different types of tuning pegs, fine tuners, and tailpieces, to how body dimensions and the bridge may influence the instrument's timbre. Tips on trying out instruments and bows are included. Special chapters are devoted to the characteristics of different types of strings, bows, and rosins, allowing you to get the most out of your instrument.

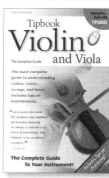

Tipbook Vocals – The Singing Voice – $14.95

Tipbook Vocals –The Singing Voice helps you realize the full potential of your singing voice. The book, written in close collaboration with classical and non-classical singers and teachers, allows you to discover the world's most personal and precious instrument without reminding you of anatomy class. Topics include breathing and breath support, singing loudly without hurting your voice, singing in tune, the timbre of your voice, articulation, registers and ranges, memorizing lyrics, and more. The main purpose of the chapter on voice care is to prevent problems.

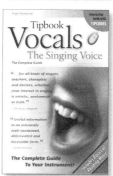

International editions

The Tipbook Series is also available in Spanish, French, German, Dutch, Italian, and Chinese. For more information, please visit us at www. tipbook.com.

Tipbook Series Music and Musical Instruments

Tipbook Acoustic Guitar
ISBN 978-1-4234-4275-2, HL00332373 — $14.95

Tipbook Amplifiers and Effects
ISBN 978-1-4234-6277-4, HL00332776 — $14.99

Tipbook Cello
ISBN 978-1-4234-5623-0, HL00331904 — $14.95

Tipbook Clarinet
ISBN 978-1-4234-6524-9, HL00332803 — $14.99

Tipbook Drums
ISBN 978-90-8767-102-0, HL00331474 — $14.95

Tipbook Electric Guitar and Bass Guitar
ISBN 978-1-4234-4274-5, HL00332372 — $14.95

Tipbook Flute and Piccolo
ISBN 978-1-4234-6525-6, HL00332804 — $14.99

Tipbook Home Keyboard and Digital Piano
ISBN 978-1-4234-4277-6, HL00332375 — $14.99

Tipbook Music for Kids and Teens
ISBN 978-1-4234-6526-3, HL00332805 — $14.99

Tipbook Music on Paper — Basic Theory
ISBN 978-1-4234-6529-4, HL00332807 — $14.99

Tipbook Piano
ISBN 978-1-4234-6278-1, HL00332777 — $14.99

Tipbook Saxophone
ISBN 978-90-8767-101-3, HL00331475 — $14.95

Tipbook Trumpet and Trombone, Flugelhorn and Cornet
ISBN 978-1-4234-6527-0, HL00332806 — $14.99

Tipbook Violin and Viola
ISBN 978-1-4234-4276-9, HL00332374 — $14.95

Tipbook Vocals — The Singing Voice
ISBN 978-1-4234-5622-3, HL00331949 — $14.95

Check www.tipbook.com for additional information!